Applications of Reading Strategies within the Classroom

Applications of Reading Strategies within the Classroom

Explanations, Models, and Teacher Templates for Content Areas in Grades 3–12

Cecilia B. Frank
Northeastern University/Webster University

Janice M. Grossi
Benedictine University, Lisle, Illinois

Dorothy J. Stanfield
Olivet Nazarene University, Bourbonaise, Illinois

PEARSON

Boston   New York   San Francisco
Mexico City   Montreal   Toronto   London   Madrid   Munich   Paris
Hong Kong   Singapore   Tokyo   Cape Town   Sydney

Senior Editor: Aurora Martínez Ramos
Series Editorial Assistant: Kevin Shannon
Senior Marketing Manager: Krista Clark
Production Editor: Annette Joseph
Editorial Production Service: Holly Crawford
Composition Buyer: Andrew Turso
Manufacturing Buyer: Andrew Turso
Electronic Composition: Peggy Cabot
Interior Design: Glenna Collett
Cover Administrator: Kristina Mose-Libon

For related titles and support materials, visit our online catalog at www.ablongman.com.

Between the time website information is gathered and then published, it is not unusual for some sites to have closed. Also, the transcription of URLs can result in typographical errors. The publisher would appreciate notification where these errors occur so that they may be corrected in subsequent editions.

Library of Congress Cataloging-in-Publication Data

Frank, Cecilia B.
    Applications of reading strategies within the classroom : explanations, models, and teacher templates for content areas in grades 3–12 / Cecilia B. Frank, Janice M. Grossi, Dorothy J. Stanfield.
       p. cm.
    ISBN 0-205-45603-0
       1. Content area reading. I. Grossi, Janice M. II. Stanfield, Dorothy J. III. Title

    LB1050.455.F72 2006
    372.47'6—dc22

                                                                      2005048936

Printed in the United States of America

10 9 8 7 6 5 4 3   VHP   09 08 07

Contents

Introduction

This book grew out of a two-year staff development project in Homewood School District 153. Just as reports indicated that reading scores had dropped nationwide, our district was experiencing concern about its own reading scores. Many teachers had limited coursework related to teaching reading in the content areas. Therefore, a consultant was hired to provide monthly inservice. Using a "train the trainers" model, all teachers were introduced to various learning strategies. While in the process of reviewing books and journal articles to determine the best strategies to present, we discovered that a more formalized and structured approach was needed to make implementation easier for classroom teachers. We wanted teachers to have a very well developed approach for teaching content area reading strategies with the opportunity for choices.

This **structured guide of strategies** not only provides teachers with practical applications, but also has the supporting research. It is written to be helpful to the staff in a school. The templates are effective teaching tools beneficial to teachers who want to facilitate students' self-directed learning. According to research, reading strategies are tied together through the process of using prior knowledge of the content and structure of text, through questioning and note taking during reading (engaged learning), and through end writing and talking (summarizing); these three components guarantee comprehension and retention. With all these components in place, we know that teachers will benefit by addressing both theory and practice. This easy-to-follow book is written with the teacher in mind, while at the same time accommodating the needs of the central and building administrators.

This "teacher friendly" manual provides the models and templates for teachers to use in planning lessons on effective learning strategies for students to understand content level materials. In a nonthreatening manner, this book offers a concise yet complete review of the research supporting each of the strategies contained here so that it can be used by teachers and administrators working with federal programs such as No Child Left Behind, Reading First, Title I, and ESL programs, as well as for IEP, resource, and challenged learners. In addition, every chapter contains a brief review of research that supports the use of strategies for each area of comprehension.

Fifty strategies are featured in what will undoubtedly become an indispensable book. Proven favorites as well as new strategies that the authors have field tested in classrooms include Stop-the-Process, Heading through a Picture Walk, THIEVES, Four-Square Reciprocal Teaching, Readers' Theater, GRASP the Headings, Partner Knowledge Rater+, and First, The Questions.

Outstanding Features:

- **Review of the research** supporting the content in each chapter will help teachers understand that research supports what they teach students.

- **A *before, during, and after* reading component** strengthens each strategy in every chapter, providing teachers with guidance for preparing lessons with students.

- All chapters are aligned with the **English Language Arts Standards (IRA/NCTE),** offering teachers a quick reference of which of their teaching strategies are aligned with which literacy standards.

- Chapter 8 demonstrates **how to integrate several strategies** for optimal learning to help teachers enhance student learning by incorporating more than one strategy in their teaching.

We hope that teachers and administrators everywhere find this book a great tool to help them guide students to become self-directed learners. We have enjoyed the collegial journey as we prepared this manuscript for other professional colleagues. We are especially grateful to Dianne Koenecke, Webster University, and Claire Ritterhoff, Goucher College, who reviewed our text for Allyn and Bacon. It is a legacy of love to promote literacy in every learning community. While we think that the book can stand alone, we also offer our expertise to others desiring assistance in improving learning and help to their staff and students. We are professionals and know that we are all part of the wider learning community helping every student to become a lifelong learner.

About the Authors

Cecilia B. Frank has been a teacher for 28 years, a graduate instructor for 25 years for Northeastern Illinois University, National-Louis University, Aurora University, and Webster University. As a literacy consultant, she presently assists schools in staff development. Cecilia holds a master's degree in Reading and Illinois certification in grades 6–12 in English and Social Science, as well as K–12 certification in Reading, Learning Disabilities, Behavior Disorders, and Supervision of Reading, Learning Disabilities, and Behavior Disorders. She is author of a study skills booklet and recently a coauthor of an article in *Educational Research Service,* Vol. 22, No. 1, "Professional Development Focuses on Learning Strategies for Content Area Readers." Cecilia has been a presenter at the Illinois Teachers of English, the Suburban Council of International Reading Association, Northwest Suburban Speech, Language and Hearing Association, Illinois Social Science Convention, and the South Cook Intermediate Service Center. She is a member of the Suburban Council of the International Reading Association, the Illinois Reading Council, the International Reading Association, the Secondary Reading League, and the State of Illinois Educational Leadership Cadre.

Janice M. Grossi has been a teacher for 25 years. She holds a master's in education degree from Governor's State University. Jan has taught reading at elementary grades, first through eighth during her career, and recently retired as Reading Specialist at Homewood, Illinois, School District #153.

Jan teaches undergrad and graduate level classes in literacy at Benedictine University. Recently, Jan has been a coauthor of several articles: "Implementing language scaffolds for struggling readers: Expansions in questioning strategies," *Illinois Reading Council Journal*, Vol. 33, No. 2, and "Professional development focuses on learning strategies for content area readers," *Educational Research Service*, Vol. 22, No. 1. Jan has been a presenter at the Illinois Reading Conference as well as the Illinois Title I Conference speaking on visual fluency yearly from 1998 to 2002. Jan has also presented "Vision for Reading: It's More than 20/20" at the South Suburban Speech, Language and Hearing Association. Jan is a member of Phi Delta Kappa, Honor Society of International Reading Association: Alpha Upsilon Alpha, International Reading Council, Illinois Reading Council, and Northern Illinois Reading Council. This is her first book. Jan is married with three children. She is a third generation teacher and her two daughters are teachers.

Dorothy J. Stanfield has been an educator for 34 years. She has been a teacher, counselor, principal, curriculum coordinator, and assistant superintendent. She earned her doctorate from Illinois State University. Dorothy is an administrator whose role includes that of grant writer, staff developer and leader for teaching and learning in Homewood School District 153. She is also a graduate instructor for a Master's Cohort in Curriculum and Instruction through Olivet Nazarene University. Professional affiliations include membership in the Association for Supervision and Curriculum Development, Illinois Association for Supervision and Curriculum Development, Phi Delta Kappa, Delta Kappa Gamma, and International Reading Association. She has presented at regional, state and national conferences on a variety of topics including reading. Her most recently published article entitled "Professional Development Focuses on Learning Strategies for Content Area Readers" was authored with Cecilia Frank and Jan Grossi through *Educational Research Service.*

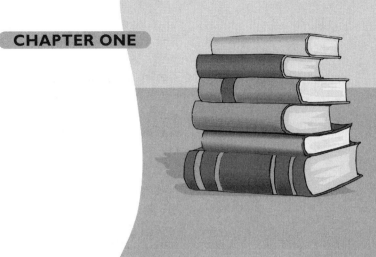

CHAPTER ONE

Foundation of Learning Strategies

Research of Strategies

Connecting

History of Strategies
Strategies Connected to
    Content Areas
Strategies Connected to
    Literacy Standards

Background

Why Teachers Use Strategies
The Origin of Strategies
Supportive Research

Application

The Importance of Modeling
    Strategies
A Case Study in Content
    Area Reading

Teachers are architects of active learning environments and place students at the center of "meaning making" in content classrooms (Vacca & Vacca, 2005). Diversity has increased, therefore traditional lecture/read, recite methods are no longer the only appropriate means of instruction. Teachers now need to use text as an important *piece* of learning while incorporating trade books, electronic text, and *varied* *strategies* to lead *all* students along the path to a lifetime of learning.

Importance of Strategies

According to the research, we know that students who naturally use learning strategies are more successful in school than those who do not (Biemiller & Meichenbaum,

1992). Generally, the gifted students automatically use strategies as they read. We realize, therefore, it is important to model the use of effective strategies within the classroom so that all students can be knowledgeable about using them. All students—whether they are English language learners, diagnosed special education, or considered slow learners—can benefit by being introduced to these strategies, but they will benefit more if these strategies are modeled and reinforced in the classroom and used across all content areas. As *all* students learn how to apply these strategies in their reading, particularly with content area materials, they will become more self-directed in their learning. This leads to more effective learners in our classrooms, which leads to greater student achievement in our schools.

The Origin of Strategies

In 1946, F. P. Robinson published the book, *Effective Study*, which provided a detailed description of the SQ3R method of study. It was from Survey, Question, Read, Recite, and Review (SQ3R) that a myriad of learning strategies evolved. By the late 1960s and early 1970s, many types of directed reading thinking lessons were presented along with structured overviews, note taking systems, study guides, and instructional frameworks. In 1970, H. L. Herber published *Teaching Reading in Content Areas,* which contained many of the original forms of learning strategies used today all over the United States. By the late 1970s, cognitive psychologists explored the effects of prior knowledge on comprehension. By the 1980s, it became apparent through research that students who took an active strategic role in their learning performed more successfully. In the 1990s and early 2000s, some teachers started using a few of the strategies that are outlined in our book. By developing a compre-

hensive manuscript that purports the theory along with practical applications regarding content area reading, the idea of providing students with independent learning through self-owned strategies evolved.

Supportive Research for Our Strategies

A large body of research supports the process and strategies presented in this book. Prior knowledge (Chapter 2) is one of the major keys to comprehension of text. The research states that students get more out of reading when their background knowledge is activated, built, or focused. This includes prereading knowledge of content, text structure, and vocabulary. Background knowledge is motivated and activated through clearly stated purposes, tasks, and prereading questions (Block & Pressley, 2001; Rumelhart, 1980; Armbruster & Anderson, 1984; Bartlett, 1978; Beck, Perfetti, & McKeown, 1982; Johnson, Toms-Bronowski, & Pittelman, 1981; Schacter, 1978; Brown, Campione, & Day, 1981; Kintsch & Van Dijk, 1978; Anderson et al., 1977; Fass & Schumacker, 1981).

The chapters on prior knowledge, instructional frames, vocabulary, talking to learn, writing to learn, studying text, and integration of strategies are supported by research that states students who are actively involved in their learning are more effective learners. Students who generate questions, take notes, make summaries and contribute to discussions, and help determine the direction of lessons are more efficient learners (Blachowicz & Ogle, 2001; Cohen, 1983; Brown, Campione, & Day, 1981; Kintsch & VanDijk, 1978; Andre & Anderson, 1979; Frase & Schwartz, 1975). The more students write and talk about what they are reading, the more they comprehend and remember what they have just read. If what is learned is not acted upon, it is quickly forgotten (Loftus, 1980; Doctorow, Wittrock, & Marks, 1978; Craik & Lockhart, 1972; Bower, 1970). The strategies in the chapters on prior knowledge, instructional frames, vocabulary, talking to learn, writing to learn, studying text, and integration of strategies all require that the students are actively presenting what they have learned through their own interpretation of the information.

Research on cooperative learning (Vacca & Vacca, 2005; Johnson & Johnson, 1985) supports the use of learning strategies, which lead to increased student achievement. The more students tutor each other, the greater their achievement. Greater learning occurs when students work together to accomplish a learning task (Dansereau, 1987; Palincsar & Brown, 1985; Slavin, 1980).

When students generate their own questions, are exposed to higher-order questions, and are asked questions about text organization, their comprehension is increased (Harvey & Goudvis, 2000; Andre & Anderson, 1979; Wixson, 1983; Redfield & Roussear, 1981). All chapters in this book involve questioning before, during, and after reading. Good high-level questions, student-generated questions about content, and questions about text structure lead to greater learning. The importance of prior knowledge; active participation through reading, writing, and talking; cooperative grouping; and good teacher and student questioning are supported by replicated research. The strategies in this book lead to student-owned strategic learning.

Why Teachers Need Strategies

As teachers plan to present content area material, as well as language arts lessons, we realized that lesson planning is no longer a simple matter. That is why having the strategies as well as the templates provided through this book is so helpful. Preparing a class presentation incorporates prereading and studying; composing and duplicating appropriate graphic organizers; activating background knowledge for student motivation and engagement; and previewing text to analyze structure and take advantage of imbedded graphs, pictures, charts, maps, and examples; and previewing end questions. The teacher then needs to determine if the lesson plan goals match the objectives of the text chosen, the outcomes of the district, and the standards of the state in which they teach as well as the national standards. The main focus is to find the "hook" for students to use as a springboard into learning.

Teachers need to suggest that students reflect as they read. Students must ask, "Is the selection following the path they initially thought?" They may need to repredict before they move on, for reading with understanding is a series of predicting, proving, disproving, and predicting again. As students read, graphic organizers, study guides, or instructional frames provide support that helps the students interact and respond to difficult texts with meaning and purpose. At the conclusion of reading, students reflect and participate in discussion through small group or class venues. All students should be able to participate on a level that is individually meaningful.

Using the strategies included in this book will be a first step for many teachers to help make learning *real* for students. GO SLOW. Be sure to model the selected strategy a time or two so students know where you are headed and what you will be expecting from them. When modeling the strategy, use an overhead if at all possible. Talk your way through the modeling and say aloud what you are thinking. State how you arrive at the answers you are selecting. Get the class involved in your modeling, use their ideas, and value their thoughts.

Teachers, however, also need to know which strategies to model if they want all of their students to become successful readers. They need assistance with which strategies to use in their curriculum and how to apply them in their classroom.

This book is designed to provide all teachers with knowledge of which strategies will work with which content areas. Resources, such as *Mosaic of Thought* (Keene & Zimmerman, 1997) present what good readers do to learn. This book gives teachers the tools to apply the directions, models, and templates to enhance their teaching process.

A chart of the various strategies that teachers can use with particular subject areas is shown below.

Strategies Connected to Content Areas

Language Arts

Anticipation Guide	Possible Sentences
Cloze	Picture Walk
Compare/Contrast Summary	Partner Knowledge Rater+
Discussion Web	Prediction Pairs
Double-Entry Journal	Proposition/Support
DRTA	Pyramid Frame
First, The Questions	QAR
Four-Step Summary	Questioning the Text
Framed Paragraphs	Radio Reading
Four-Square Reciprocal	RAFT
Teaching	Readers' Theater
GIST	Response Journal
GRASP	Stop-the-Process
Inquiry-Chart	Story Impression
Jigsaw	Story Map
KWL+	THIEVES
KWLH+	Think-Aloud
List-Group-Label	Think-Aloud
Magic Squares	with Questions

Foreign Language

Anticipation Guide	Picture Walk
Cloze	Partner Knowledge Rater+
Compare/Contrast Summary	Prediction Pairs
Discussion Web	Proposition/Support
Double-Entry Journal	Pyramid Frame
DRTA	QAR
First, The Questions	Questioning the Text
Four-Step Summary	Radio Reading
Framed Paragraphs	RAFT
Four-Square Reciprocal	Readers' Theater
Teaching	Response Journal
GIST	RIVET
GRASP	Semantic Feature Analysis
Inquiry-Chart	Stop-the-Process
Jigsaw	Story Impression
KWL+	Story Map
KWLH+	Think-Aloud
List-Group-Label	Think-Aloud
Magic Squares	with Questions
Possible Sentences	

Mathematics

Anticipation Guide	Heading through a
Carousel Brainstorming	Picture Walk
Compare/Contrast	Inquiry-Chart
Organizer	Magnet Summaries
Concept Circles	QAR
Concept Diagram	RAFT
Discussion Web	Response Journal
Double-Entry Journal	Semantic Feature Analysis
First, The Questions	SQ3R
Four-Step Summary	Stop-the-Process
Frayer Model	Two-Column Notes
Framed Paragraph	Word Map
GIST	

Physical Education

Anticipation Guide	Partner Knowledge Rater+
Compare/Contrast	Proposition/Support
Organizer	Pyramid Frame
Discussion Web	QAR
First, The Questions	Question the Text
Four-Step Summary	RAFT
Framed Paragraphs	Response Journal
GIST	RIVET
Heading through a	Semantic Feature Analysis
Picture Walk	Stop-the-Process
Inquiry-Chart	Text Impression
KWLH+	Think-Aloud
List-Group-Label	with Questions
Magic Squares	Two-Column Notes
Magnet Summaries	Word Map

Science and Health

Anticipation Guide	Critical Thinking Summary
Carousel Brainstorming	Discussion Web
Classification Organizer	Double Entry Journal
Compare/Contrast	First, The Questions
Organizer	Four-Square Reciprocal
Cloze	Teaching
Concept Circles	Four-Step Summary
Concept Diagram	Framed Paragraphs

Science and Health (continued)

Frayer Model	Proposition/Support
GIST	Pyramid Frame
GRASP	QAR
Heading through a Picture Walk	Question the Text
	RAFT
Inquiry-Chart	Response Journal
Internal Text Structure/ Notes and Frames	RIVET
	Semantic Feature Analysis
Jigsaw	SQ3R
KWLH+	Stop-the-Process
List-Group-Label	Text Impression
Magic Squares	THIEVES
Magnet Summaries	Think-Aloud with Questions
Partner Knowledge Rater+	
Picture Walk	Two-Column Notes
Possible Sentences	Word Map

Social Science

Anticipation Guide	Jigsaw
Carousel Brainstorming	KWLH+
Classification Organizer	List-Group-Label
Compare/Contrast Organizer	Magic Squares
	Magnet Summaries
Cloze	Partner Knowledge Rater+
Concept Circles	Picture Walk
Concept Diagram	Possible Sentences
Critical Thinking Summary	Proposition/Support
Discussion Web	Pyramid Frame
Double Entry Journal	QAR
First, The Questions	Question the Text
Four-Square Reciprocal Teaching	RAFT
	Response Journal
Four-Step Summary	RIVET
Framed Paragraphs	Semantic Feature Analysis
Frayer Model	SQ3R
GIST	Stop-the-Process
GRASP	Text Impression
Heading through a Picture Walk	THIEVES
	Think-Aloud with Questions
Inquiry-Chart	
Internal Text Structure/ Notes and Frames	Two-Column Notes
	Word Map

Fine Arts: Music, Art, Drama

Anticipation Guide	Partner Knowledge Rater+
Compare/Contrast Organizer	Picture Walk
	Possible Sentences
Cloze	Prediction Pairs
Concept Circles	Proposition/Support
Concept Diagram	Pyramid Frame
Discussion Web	QAR
Double-Entry Journal	Question the Text
First, The Questions	Radio Reading
Four-Step Summary	RAFT
Framed Paragraph	Readers' Theater
Frayer Model	Response Journal
GIST	RIVET
GRASP	Stop-the-Process
KWL+	Story Impressions
KWLH+	Story Map
Jigsaw	Think-Aloud with Questions
List-Group-Label	
Magic Squares	Two-Column Notes
Magnet Summaries	

Technology

Anticipation Guide	KWLH+
Carousel Brainstorming	List-Group-Label
Classification Organizer	Magnet Summaries
Compare/Contrast Organizer	Partner Knowledge Rater+
	Picture Walk
Cloze	Proposition/Support
Concept Circles	QAR
Concept Diagram	Question the Text
Discussion Web	RAFT
Double-Entry Journal	Response Journal
First, The Questions	RIVET
Four-Step Summary	Semantic Feature Analysis
Framed Paragraphs	SQ3R
Frayer Model	Stop-the-Process
GIST	THIEVES
GRASP	Think-Aloud with Questions
Heading through a Picture Walk	
	Two-Column Notes
Inquiry-Chart	Word Map
Internal Text Structure/ Notes and Frames	

Teachers also need to make sure that they are teaching to appropriate national, state, and local standards. The following chart shows the relationship of the content area learning strategies the authors felt were related to the Standards for the English Language Arts as well as the impact that this application has on student learning (NCTE & IRA, 1996):

Learning Strategies Connected to Literacy Standards

Wide and Varied Reading

Students read a wide range of print and nonprint texts to build understanding and comprehension (NCTE/IRA, 1996, p. 3).

Sources

Electronic Text
Libraries
Media Centers
Text Books
Trade Books

Strategies

Anticipation Guide
Cloze
Compare/Contrast,
  Graphic and Summary
Concept Circles
Concept Diagram
Critical Thinking Summary
Discussion Web
Double-Entry Journal
First, The Questions
Four-Step Summary
Four-Square Reciprocal
  Teaching
Frayer Model
GIST
GRASP the Headings
Incomplete Framed
  Paragraphs
Inquiry-Chart
Internal Text Structure and
  Notes
Heading through a
  Picture Walk
Jigsaw
KWL+
KWLH+
List-Group-Label

Magic Squares
Magnet Summaries
Partner Knowledge Rater+
Picture Walk
Possible Sentences
Prediction Pairs
Proposition/Support
Pyramid Frame
QAR
Question the Text
Radio Reading
RAFT
Response Journal
RIVET
Seed Discussion
Semantic Feature Analysis
Stop-the-Process
Story Map
Text Impression
THIEVES
Think-Aloud
Think-Aloud
  with Questions
Think-Pair-Share
Two-Column Notes
Word Map

Varied Genre

Students read a wide range of literature from many periods in many genres to build understanding (NCTE/IRA, 1996, p. 3).

Sources

Anthologies
Electronic Text
Libraries
Media Centers
Text Books
Trade Books

Strategies

Anticipation Guide
Cloze

Possible Sentences
Prediction Pairs

Compare/Contrast,
  Graphic and Summary
Discussion Web
Double-Entry Journal
DRTA
First, The Questions
Four-Step Summary
Four-Square Reciprocal
  Teaching
GIST
Incomplete Framed
  Paragraphs
Inquiry-Chart
Jigsaw
KWL+
KWLH+
List-Group-Label
Magic Squares
Partner Knowledge Rater+
Picture Walk

Proposition/Support
Pyramid Frame
QAR
Question the Text
Radio Reading
RAFT
Readers' Theater
Response Journal
Seed Discussion
Stop-the-Process
Story Impression
Story Map
Themed Reading
  Units
Think-Aloud
Think-Aloud
  with Questions
Think-Pair-Share
Word Map

Wide Range of Strategies

Students apply a wide range of strategies to comprehend, interpret, evaluate, and appreciate texts (NCTE/IRA, 1996, p. 3).

Before Reading

Anticipation Guide
Directed-Reading-
  Thinking-Activity
First, The Questions
Heading through a
  Picture Walk
KWL+
KWLH+

Picture Walk
Possible Sentences
Prediction Pairs
Story Impressions
THIEVES
Think-Aloud
Think-Aloud
  with Questions

During Interaction with Text

Concept Diagrams
Critical Thinking Questions
Double-Entry Journal
Four-Square Reciprocal
  Teaching
Graphic Organizers
GRASP the Headings
Internal Text Structures

Proposition/Support
Question the Text
Seed Discussion
SQ3R
Stop-the-Process
Story Map
Text Talk
Two-Column Notes

After Reading, Writing, Talking

Critical Thinking Summary
Discussion Web
Incomplete Paragraph
  Frames
Four-Step Summary
GIST
GRASP the Headings
Inquiry-Chart
Jigsaw

Question the Text
Pyramid Frames
Radio Reading
RAFT
Readers' Theater
Response Journal
Seed Discussion
Semantic Feature Analysis

Vocabulary

Classification and
    Categorization
Cloze Procedure
Concept Circles
Frayer Model
List-Group-Label
Magic Squares
Magnet Summaries

Partner Knowledge Rater+
Possible Sentences
RIVET
Semantic Feature Analysis
Story Impressions
Think-Pair-Share
Word Map

Communications: Spoken, Written, Visual

Students adjust their use of spoken, written, and
visual language (e.g., conventions, style, vocabulary)
to communicate effectively with a variety of
audiences and for different purposes (NCTE/IRA,
1996, p. 3).

Strategies

Carousel Brainstorming
Concept Diagram
Critical Reading Summary
Discussion Web
Double-Entry Journal
Four-Square Reciprocal
    Teaching
Four-Step Summary
GIST
GRASP the Headings
Incomplete Paragraph
    Frames
Inquiry-Chart
Jigsaw

Proposition/Support
Pyramid Frame
Radio Reading
RAFT
Reader/Response
Readers' Theater
Response Journal
Seed Discussion
Stop-the-Process
Story Map
Text Talk
THIEVES
Think-Pair-Share
Two-Column Notes

Wide Range of Writing Strategies

Students employ a wide range of strategies as they
write and use different writing elements appropriately to communicate with different audiences for a
variety of purposes (NCTE/IRA, 1996, p. 3).

Strategies

Exploratory Writing

Double-Entry Journals
Possible Sentences
Proposition/Support
RAFT
Response Journal

Seed Discussion
Story Impressions
Text Impressions
Text Talk
Two-Column Notes

Summary Writing (Standard)

Concept Diagram
Critical Thinking Summary
Discussion Web
Four-Square Reciprocal
    Teaching
Four-Step Summary
Framed Paragraphs
GIST
GRASP the Headings

Heading through a
    Picture Walk
KWLH+
Pyramid Frame
Semantic Feature Analysis
Story Impressions
Story Map
Text Impressions

Essay Writing and Research

Inquiry-Chart
Questions, Organize, First Draft, Public Writing
Six Steps: Local Subject, Notetaking, Organization, First
    Draft, Respond and Revise, Publish, Evaluate and Grade

Knowledge of Language Structure and Conventions

Students apply knowledge of language structure,
language conventions (e.g., spelling and punctua-
tion), media techniques, figurative language, and
genre to create, critique, and discuss print and
nonprint texts. Teacher expectations dictate that all
strategies require proper use of grammar, usage,
rhetoric, and mechanics (NCTE/IRA, 1996, p. 3).

Strategies

Carousel Brainstorming
Concept Circles
Concept Diagram
Critical Reading Summary
Discussion Web
Double-Entry Journal
Four-Square Reciprocal
    Teaching
Four-Step Summary
GIST
GRASP the Headings
Incomplete Paragraph
    Frames
Inquiry-Chart
Jigsaw
Possible Sentences

Proposition/Support
Pyramid Frame
Radio Reading
RAFT
Reader/Response
Readers' Theater
Response Journal
Seed Discussion
Stop-the-Process
Story Impressions
Story Map
Text Impressions
Text Talk
Think-Pair-Share
Two-Column Notes

Research: Gather, Evaluate, and Synthesize Data

Students conduct research on issues and interests
by generating ideas and questions, and by posing
problems. They gather, evaluate, and synthesize data
from a variety of sources (e.g., print and nonprint
texts, artifacts, people) to communicate their
discoveries in ways that suit their purposes and
audience (NCTE/IRA, 1996, p. 3).

Strategies

Critical Thinking Summary
Discussion Web
Double-Entry Jounral
Four-Square Reciprocal
    Teaching
GRASP the Headings
Inquiry/Research Focus
    (Inquiry Chart and
    I Wonder Charts)
Internal Text Structures
Jigsaw

KWLH+
Magnet Summaries
Picture Walk
Picture Walk
    with Headings
Question the Text
Response Journal
Semantic Feature Analysis
THIEVES
Two-Column Notes
Word Maps

The Importance of Modeling Strategies

Once teachers gain an understanding of the strategies that have been identified as important through the research, they can model with students. Since they are now knowledgeable of which ones apply to specific content areas as well as the national standards, teachers are empowered to create their own lessons that integrate learning. Students will be able to acquire the knowledge to meet their learning goals as identified through the standards movement. As teachers integrate state and local goals with the lesson objectives through repeated applications of the learning strategies in the classroom, the students will ultimately show gains in student achievement on local, state, and national assessments.

This book presents the research that supports various learning strategies for teachers to incorporate in their classroom. It also presents examples of tried and true lessons that have been modeled by professionals with students. It gives staff members templates that they can use to design their instruction. By combining sound theory with effective practice, teachers are assured of success in preparing students for self-directed learning.

A Case Study in Content Area Reading

At the end of the two-year staff development process, we evaluated our overall progress in teaching content area learning strategies. We posed the question, "Was our plan to provide staff development in content area reading strategies actually providing students with the tools they needed to be successful learners?" We used qualitative research to arrive at an answer by triangulating the data from teacher surveys, the Illinois Standards Achievement Test results, and informal observations in the classrooms by the administrators in each school. The teachers across the district had many positive comments to make about the use of strategies and about the impact the strategies had on student learning. A sampling is provided next:

- "The time invested in working through a strategy is time well spent. Students are more involved in the subject matter and retain the information longer."

- "I no longer teach Science or Social Studies without some type of strategy. I think the reading strategies are that valuable."

- "The biggest area of growth was in vocabulary retention. Students scored far better on words for which a vocabulary strategy was employed than on words that we simply reviewed orally."

- "Using GIST helped students dramatically to gain the "key" concepts of the chapter—as long as I keep the sections brief."

- "Students *know how* to preview a content area lesson."

- "Students automatically reread sections in Social Studies and Science when they can't answer the focus question."

- "At the beginning of the year when I was using a strategy in Science, a student asked 'Are you going to teach Science like this all year?' I explained how we were using reading strategies. She said, 'Wow this is easy!' What a wonderful comment about learning."

- "Stop The Process helped many of my students who were struggling with comprehension. My students have evolved into readers who have now learned to think critically about the material."

- "The reading strategies refreshed my lesson plans and provided so many opportunities for my students to be successful."

A comparison of the Illinois Standards Achievement Test over the past two years was made to show indicators of increased student success. The charts are shown below:

Homewood, Illinois School District 153
Illinois Standard Achievement Tests
Performance Level Percentages
3rd Grade Reading

School Year	Academic Warning	Below Standards	Meets Standards	Exceeds Standards
2002	2	18	53	27
2001	3	24	50	24

Note: At the third grade level, 80% of our students met or exceeded the Illinois Learning Standards during the 2002 school year as measured on the Illinois Standard Achievement Test as compared to 74% the previous year. Only 18% of our students were below standards in the 2002 school year as compared to 24% the year before.

5th Grade Reading

School Year	Academic Warning	Below Standards	Meets Standards	Exceeds Standards
2002	0	21	42	37
2001	0	25	39	35

Note: At the fifth grade level, 79% of our students met or exceeded the Illinois Learning Standards as measured on the Illinois Standard Achievement Test during the 2002 school year as compared to 74% the prior year. Only 21% of our students scored below standards during the 2002 school year as compared to 25% the year before.

This information gave us some indication that student scores were increasing in the meets and exceeds categories and decreasing for the academic warning and below standards categories. Finally, informal observations of teachers in the classroom by administrators proved that a unique environment for student learning was being created.

Conclusion

The teachers were looking at text in new ways—they now had tools to scaffold student learning—and content area reading was becoming "interesting" and "fun" for them. A few of the teachers felt that the strategies were a lot of work—and they were—but the majority of the teachers were excited and empowered by the new strategies they had learned. To observe the lessons and listen to the overwhelmingly positive comments from teachers at every level reflecting on the fact that students were enjoying their work and retaining the text information longer when strategies were employed was incredible!

The triangulation of our data, regarding the surveys, observations, and achievement test comparison scores indicated that positive results were occurring in the district. Although we can never assume that any qualitative research study be transferred to any other situation, we can report the positive results we feel were achieved in Homewood.

We can only predict that school districts engaged in using *Applications of Reading Strategies within the Classroom* will increase student achievement. By providing Explanations, Models, and Teacher Templates for content areas in grades three through twelve, students can become self-directed learners.

CHAPTER TWO

Prior Knowledge

Prior Knowledge Strategies

Connecting
KWLH+
KWL
Story Impressions—Nonfiction
Story Impressions Chart—
  Fiction

Curiosity and Background
Anticipation Guide
Picture Walk
Heading through a Picture
  Walk
Think-Aloud

Questioning
Think-Aloud with Questions
First, The Questions

R aising expectations and generating interest about the text's meaning naturally creates a context, which enables students to read with purpose and anticipation (Vacca & Vacca, 2005).

Research Preview
Recent research stresses if the students have prior knowledge before reading then comprehension will be increased. The more information that a student has about the content, the clearer the text will become. Based on the research of Anderson and Pearson (1984), the National Reading Panel Report (February, 2000) states, "Schema theory holds that comprehension depends upon the integration of new knowledge with a network of prior knowledge." It is helpful for the teacher to provide background information if they sense that the

students do not have adequate information. This provides a building block for greater understanding of the content materials that students encounter in today's classrooms.

English Language Arts Standard

Students apply a wide range of strategies to comprehend, interpret, evaluate, and appreciate texts. They draw on their prior experience, their interactions with other readers and writers, their knowledge of word meaning and of other texts, their word identification strategies, and their understanding of textual features (NCTE and IRA, 1996, p. 25).

Connections to Research

Comprehension has been defined as "Building bridges between the new and the known" (Pearson & Johnson, 1978, p. 24). "Prior knowledge is a combination of culture, context, and experience—not just a collection of facts, but also an understanding of relationships among concepts and principles" (North Central Regional Educational Laboratory, 2000, p. 53). The established information, known as prior knowledge, is the foundation upon which the new information builds. Without appropriate prior knowledge, a reader cannot draw relevant inferences. This prior knowledge has been derived from schema theory (Anderson & Pearson, 1984).

Schema provides a framework for seeking and selecting information that is relevant to the purpose of reading. It allows the reader to make inferences about the text. Inferences occur where you anticipate content and text structure and make predictions.

A schema helps the reader organize text information. This process allows the reader to organize and integrate new information into an old knowledge structure or prior knowledge. This gives the reader the ability to retain and remember the new and old information.

A schema helps elaborate upon information. The reader uses deeper levels of thinking, insight, judgment, and evaluation. The reader literally engages in a conversation with the author. According to Pearson, Roehler, Dole, and Duffy (Samuels & Farstrup, 1992), research studies have emphasized the following:

1. Students with greater prior knowledge comprehend and remember more (Brown et al., 1977; Pearson, Hansen, & Gordon, 1979).

2. Merely having prior knowledge is not enough to improve comprehension; the knowledge must be activated, implying a strong metacognitive dimension to its use (Bransford & Johnson, 1972).

3. Young readers and poor readers often do not activate their prior knowledge (Paris & Lindauer, 1976).

4. Good readers use their prior knowledge to determine the importance of information in the text (Afflerbach, 1986).

5. Good readers use their prior knowledge to draw inferences from and elaborate on text (Gordon & Pearson, 1983; Hansen & Pearson, 1983).

This research information emphasizes the importance of using reading strategies that engage students in activating prior knowledge or building their knowledge base prior to reading.

When reading content materials, there are three types of prior knowledge that students should consider (Griggs & Gil-Garcia, 2001). The first is topic knowledge, which means having knowledge that is relevant or accurate about the topic. If the student has inaccurate information or misconceptions, it is very important that these be changed prior to reading. The second type of prior knowledge relates to text structure and organization. Students need to know how the text is organized in order to relate to the narrative or expository text. The third type of prior knowledge relates to understanding the vocabulary in content area reading materials. This helps students learn unfamiliar words and develop strategies for identifying new words.

Prior knowledge comes from many sources. These include television, radio, trips, parents, grandparents, peers, teachers, neighbors, books, and movies. Students could construct a class map to illustrate how members have learned about content materials prior to reading a selection.

Some general techniques that students can use before, during, or after reading to activate prior knowledge, evaluate what they are reading, and review how effectively they have incorporated their prior knowledge during reading are outlined below (Griggs & Gil-Garcia, 2001):

Before Reading

- Preview the content area material to be read.
- Look at the cover, pictures, title of chapter, and text.
- Discuss what students know about the above elements.
- Connect past personal experiences, observations, and knowledge obtained from various sources with new knowledge to be taught and learned.
- Look for familiar vocabulary words.
- Examine ways in which the text is organized and structured.

During Reading

- Assist students in applying their prior knowledge.
- Brainstorm ideas regarding where, how, and when students' prior knowledge can be accessed.
- Model how one's prior knowledge can be applied to unknown materials and

information to assist in learning new information and concepts.

- Encourage the use of inferencing skills as students test the application of prior knowledge.
- Correct inaccurate prior knowledge.

After Reading

- Evaluate how effectively students are able to use their prior knowledge to make connections between what they know and what they are trying to learn.
- Have students write, create graphic organizers, or make oral presentations to demonstrate their understanding of designated learning tasks.

These ideas are further elaborated with specific prior knowledge strategies that teachers can introduce to students in the classroom. Many of these strategies can be incorporated with language arts, math, science, and social studies. As students learn how to use these strategies to read content area materials, their comprehension will increase. Prior knowledge is 40 to 60 percent of a person's comprehension. This makes it extremely important for teachers to assist students in learning how to utilize prior knowledge strategies before, during, and after reading. While some good readers already employ some of these strategies, they may learn additional ones. Poor readers really need not only to be introduced to the prior knowledge strategies but also to be actively engaged in applying these strategies to their reading. This chapter outlines specific strategies for teachers to incorporate in their instruction of content area materials.

In order to generate interest and create a context where students will read content material with questions and curiosity, prior knowledge must be activated. Various prior knowledge strategies can be utilized to enhance comprehension and interest. These strategies can be tied to content areas such as math, science, and social science as well as language arts. Examples of the following strategies and their relationship to various content areas provide the scaffolding necessary for instruction.

KWL is an acronym for *Know, Want to Know, and Learned* (Carr & Ogle, 1987). According to Doug Buehl (2003), this strategy involves using a three-column graphic organizer. This strategy encourages students to become active thinkers while reading. The active reader makes predictions about what they will be reading. Before starting, active readers consider what they already know about the story or topic. As they read, they confirm whether or not their predictions were on target. Active readers have an idea of what to look for, and when they are done they evaluate what they have learned or experienced. In the first column, readers list what they already know about the story or topic. In the second column, they write the questions they want answered by the article or story. In the third column, they list the information they learned from the article or story. In our **KWLH+,** active readers organize the material by heading if it is nonfiction and by a story map if it is fiction—thus organizing their thoughts and creating associations and connections. In order to tie this strategy to the science or social science content areas, some examples include the use of chapter headings and subheadings as topics for brainstorming the student's prior knowledge. This refers to the first step or known column in the KWLH+ strategy (Frank, 1999). In math, use the numbered sample problems as the topics for brainstorming possible solutions to the problem.

Story Impressions (McGinley & Denner, 1987) is a prereading strategy that arouses curiosity and allows the students to anticipate what stories might be about. It can just as easily be used as "Text Impressions" where the key concept words arouse curiosity and allow students to anticipate an informational text. In language arts, a **Story**

Impressions Chart uses clue words associated with setting, characters, and events in the story to help readers write their own versions of the story prior to reading. After reading the set of clues, the students are asked to create their own comprehensible story in advance of reading the actual tale. The clue words are selected directly from the story and are sequenced with arrows or lines to form a descriptive chain. In science and social science, nonfiction or text impression use concept words from the title, subtitles, bold print, pictures, and captions. These clue words are presented in the order of the text. After reading the set of clues and possibly looking at the pictures and captions, the students write a paragraph describing what the chapter will cover. **Prior knowledge** is based on **schema theory.** This theory acknowledges that if an individual has a concept of a topic and its organization prior to reading, comprehension will be enhanced. Each of the strategies in this chapter focuses the students' attention on what they already know about the content and its structure.

An **Anticipation Guide** is a series of statements to which students must respond individually before reading the text (Herber, 1978; Moore et al., 1989; Readence et al., 1989; Vacca & Vacca, 2005). The value lies in the discussion that takes place after the exercise. As students connect their knowledge of the world to the prediction task, the teacher must remain open to a wide range of responses. Anticipation guides vary in format but not in purpose. In each case, the readers' expectations about meaning are raised before they read the text. To create a good anticipation guide in science, social science, math, or language arts, the teacher must analyze the material and determine the major ideas, both implicit and explicit. From the chapter's objectives listed in the teacher's manual, a series of statements can be created. These ideas must be written in short, clear declarative statements. There should be no abstractions, but instead clear statements that reflect the world in which the students live. After the students read the text, they evaluate the statements in light of the author's intent and purpose. In other words, they grade their own anticipation guides to see if their predictions are correct.

A **Picture Walk** is from the survey part of Francis Robinson's 1946 **SQ3R strategy** (Survey, Question, Read, Recite, and Review). A Picture Walk is simply a careful look through a piece of fiction or nonfiction, reading all the details in pictures and captions, in addition to reading all the titles, subtitles, and bold print. The teacher can also choose to review the end questions with the students. This is all done before reading. The students then predict what the story or chapter will be about. The teacher records these predictions on the board. The students read to verify, reject, or refine their predictions. After reading, the students compose a summary of the actual content in science, social science, language arts, and math. **Heading through a Picture Walk** (Frank, 2002) activates background knowledge by focusing on text headings.

Using **Think-Alouds,** teachers make their thinking explicit by verbalizing their thoughts while reading orally. Davey (1983) explained that this process helps readers clarify their understanding of reading and their understanding of how to use strategies. Students will more clearly understand the strategies after a teacher uses Think-Alouds because they can see how a mind actively responds to thinking through trouble spots and constructing meaning from text. Think-Alouds can be used in science, social science, math, and language arts. Davey (1983) suggested four basic steps when using Think-Alouds:

1. Select passages to read aloud that contain points of difficulty, ambiguities, contradictions, or unknown words.

2. While orally reading and modeling thinking aloud, have students follow silently and listen to how trouble spots are thought through.

3. Have students work with partners to practice Think-Alouds by taking turns reading short, carefully prepared passages and sharing thoughts.

4. Have students practice independently using a checklist.

For a **Think-Aloud with Questions,** the teacher and the students stop to verbally think aloud during the reading of the first few paragraphs of nonfiction (Frank, 2001). The students discuss and record answers to the following questions while reading language arts, science, social science, and math:

What do you now know about _____?

What information will be given in the text?

What questions do you have?

What questions will be answered by the text?

After the teacher and the students stop to think aloud during the reading of the first few paragraphs of fiction, the students answer the following questions.

Who are the characters?

What is the setting?

What is the main character's problem?

How do you think the main character's problem will be resolved?

DRTA identifies a standard *Directed Reading Thinking Activity* (Stauffer, 1969). This is an excellent strategy to get students to make inferences while reading. Students are guided through a selection to help them formulate questions and make predictions. As they read, students validate or reject their predictions.

In language arts, the standard DRTA is most effective for use with fiction. The following steps are recommended:

1. Activate background knowledge. The students look at the pictures and the title on the first page of the selection, think about what they already know about the topic, and share the ideas with others in the class.

2. Predict and set a purpose. The group predicts what the selection will be about when the teacher asks, "What do you think will happen next?" "Why do you think so?" "What evidence do you find to support your prediction?"

3. Read the selection silently. The teacher reminds students to keep their predictions and purposes in mind as they read. In many cases, it is best if the teacher places the predictions on the board in front of the room.

4. Confirm or reject the predictions. The teacher asks, "What predictions can you prove?" "Why or why not?"

5. Repeat the cycle with the next section of the text.

In science, social science, and language arts, a modified DRTA, **First, The Questions** (Frank, 1996) uses the questions at the end of the selection:

1. The students are handed a sheet with the end questions or are told to go to the end questions in the book. The students are asked to independently record a short answer to each question.

2. The students then share their answers with a partner and during this process they must come to a consensus on what the exact answer should be.

3. The teacher then records on the board the students' answers to the prereading questions.

4. Read the selection silently. The teacher reminds students to keep their predictions and purposes in mind as they read.

5. Confirm or reject the predictions. The teacher asks, "What predictions can you prove?" "Why or why not?

EXPLANATION FOR APPLICATION OF READING STRATEGY

KWLH+

KWL (Carr & Ogle, 1987) and **KWLH+** (Frank, 1999) encourage students to focus on recalling "known" information about the topic they are about to study. Teachers are also able to gain information to determine what students "want" to learn on this topic and have a means to identify what is "learned" as a result of their reading. The "plus" asks that students end the exercise by summarizing information on the topic. Creating summaries is a challenge to many students and this format allows practice for this skill.

The KWL included is a graphic organizer that can be used with ESL or struggling readers and will require some cutting and folding before use. Once the paper is cut and folded in half, the panels can be lifted. Information is recorded on the inside. Teachers can guide summary writing on the back of the pamphlet.

Before Reading

Students will use **H** text headings and prior knowledge to predict content. Brainstorm and discuss what students know about each text heading. Write information on the chalkboard or a transparency for all to view. Students consider all the discussed prior knowledge, then note their knowledge of the text heading under the **K** on the worksheet. Questions will arise from the prereading discussion and from thinking about the anticipated information in text. These questions form the **W,** which expresses what the students want to learn.

During Reading

It is best to model this strategy several times so students are comfortable with the procedure and realize the steps and processes involved. First, read a section of the material and record new information under appropriate headings. Guide students into generating questions as they read. As students read and learn, additional questions may be added to the **W** section. Students constantly think about what they read, monitor their learning, and learn to generate additional questions to guide their reading.

After Reading

Students will share information on their **KWLH+** graphic organizer with a partner. Using the headings and the recorded information, students write a summary sentence for each category, which leads a well written paragraph.

KWLH+

Topic: Early Explorers to America (1497–1610)		
K (Known)	**W** (Want to Know)	**L** (Learned)
List the headings and guess in pencil what will be stated in the subsections.	Make questions out of the headings.	As you read, take notes in pen. Add or correct the information you wrote in pencil.
H *The Voyage of John Cabot*	Where did John Cabot go on his voyage?	<u>The Voyage of John Cabot</u> To find route to Asia Landed Newfoundland, 1497 Northwest Passage
H *French Explorers*	Who were the French explorers?	<u>French Explorers</u> Jacque Cartier, 1534 Sailed up St. Lawrence river Samuel deChamplain Started settlement, 1609
H *Henry Hudson's Voyages* **H** *Dutch Explorer*	Where did Henry Hudson go on his voyages?	<u>Henry Hudson's Voyages</u> Sailed Hudson River, 1609 Sailed a Canadian bay, 1610 Now Hudson's Bay

+ Summary: John Cabot hoped to find a route to Asia. He landed in Newfoundland in 1497, thinking he found the Northwest passage. French explorers include Jacque Cartier, who sailed up the St. Lawrence River in 1534, and Samuel Champlain, who started a settlement in 1609. Henry Hudson, a Dutch explorer sailed the Hudson river in 1609 and in 1610 found the Hudson Bay.

KWLH+

Topic: _____		
K **(Known)**	**W** **(Want to Know)**	**L** **(Learned)**
List the headings and guess in pencil what will be stated in the subsections.	**Make questions out of the headings.**	**As you read, take notes in pen. Add or correct the information you wrote in pencil.**
Subheading 1:	Subheading 1:	
Subheading 2:	Subheading 2:	
Subheading 3:	Subheading 3:	

Summary: Write a sentence summary for each heading. The sentence summary should answer the question made from the subheading. Combine the sentence summaries into a paragraph summary of the chapter.

Directions: Using scissors, cut the two heavy vertical lines to the halfway mark. Then fold your sheet in half. Lift each panel and write your information for each section. (Suggested applications: ESL, struggling readers, LD resource.)

KWL

(Fold page in half on this line.)

What I	What I	What I
Know	**Want** to find out	**Learned**

Story Impressions

Story Impressions (McGinley & Denner, 1987) are a great way to arouse curiosity for reading a selection while encouraging students to anticipate the text. Clue words from the story as well as setting, characters, and events help to give the student an "impression" of the story. Words, including vocabulary, can be written sequentially with arrows or lines to form a descriptive chain. This chain of clue words will trigger some type of mental impression, which in turn allows students to write a "story guess."

Before Reading

Introduce the strategy by alerting students to the fact that their task will be to "make up" a story using selected clues. Read the clues together and explain that the arrows link one clue to the next in a logical order.

Brainstorm some story ideas that could connect the clues in the order presented and ask what they think the story could be about.

Demonstrate how to write a story guess by using the ideas generated to compose a class-generated story linking all the clues. This could be executed on an overhead for all to see.

During Reading

Students read the actual story silently alone or in a small group.

After Reading

Have students discuss the class-composed prediction compared to the author's story. How are they alike? How are they different?

Story Impressions

(Nonfiction)

Corps of Discovery

Directions: Look at the following list of words and phrases taken from the chapter on exploring western lands. The arrows link the words in a logical order. Brainstorm and write a paragraph describing the information that will be given in this chapter. Use the words and phrases from the story chain below to write the story.

Story Chain	Story Guesses
Thomas Jefferson ↓ expedition ↓ western lands ↓ Meriwether Lewis ↓ William Clark ↓ Corps of Discovery ↓ Missouri River ↓ journals ↓ notes and maps ↓ plants and wildlife ↓ Mandans ↓ Sacagawea ↓ Shoshone ↓ Snake River ↓ Columbia River ↓ Pacific Ocean	President Thomas Jefferson wanted to have an expedition to explore the western lands of the country. He sent Meriwether Lewis and William Clark to lead the Corps of Discovery. They led their group up the Missouri River. They had to keep journals, make maps, and keep notes about plants and wildlife they came across. The Mandan tribe helped the explorers. They met a trader and his wife, Sacagawea, who showed them the way. She was a Shoshone. The explorers followed the Snake River and the Columbia River to reach the Pacific Ocean.

Story Impressions

(Nonfiction)

Directions: Look at the following list of words and phrases taken from the chapter/text. The arrows link the words in a logical order. Brainstorm and write a paragraph describing the information that will be given in this chapter. Use the words and phrases sequentially from the story chain below to write the story.

Story Chain   **Story Guesses**

↓   _____

↓   _____

↓   _____

↓   _____

↓   _____

↓   _____

↓   _____

Story Impressions Chart

(Fiction)

"Dr. Heidegger's Experiment"

The teacher creates a "Story Impressions" worksheet, using words about the setting, characters, problem, events, and ending. All the words need to be pronounced aloud.

1. The teacher and the students look at the pictures in the text and read the first three or four paragraphs of the story.
2. Using the "filled in" Story Impressions Chart, the students each create a story using as many of the words as they can. Then the students share their stories with their partners or the class.

Setting	Characters	Problem	Events	Ending
house	strange unfortunate	old rose crumble	liquid	young again
laboratory	Mr. Gascon politician dishonest	experiment	fresh, lovely rose	fighting
spider webs	Mr. Medbourne fortune greedy	count on	centuries	old again
bookcases	Colonel Killigrew soldier sick	fountain of youth	astonished surprise	
	Widow Wycherly conceited wrinkled face		drink	

Example: Strange and unfortunate characters reside in the crumbling rose-colored house. Mr. Gascon, a dishonest politician spent his time on experiments to retain a rose, lovely and fresh in the laboratory. Mr. Medbourne was a greedy, yet fortunate spider. Colonel Killigrew, a sick lonely soldier, searched the bookcases for a book on the fountain of youth while Widow Wycherly with her conceited-looking, yet wrinkled old face continued to drink and encourage his efforts.

Note: Information from *English Yes!* by Burton Goodman, 2004, Columbus, OH: McGraw-Hill.

Story Impressions Chart

(Fiction)

Story Title: _____

The teacher and the students look at the pictures in the text and read the first three or four paragraphs of the story.

   Using words about the setting, characters, problem, events, and ending, fill in the following Story Impressions Chart.

   Then, using the "filled in" Story Impressions Chart, the students each create a story using as many of the words as they can. Then the students share their stories with their partners or the class.

Setting	Characters	Problem	Events	Ending

Example:

Anticipation Guide

An Anticipation Guide (Herber, 1978; Moore et al., 1989; Readence, 1989; Vacca & Vacca, 2005) uses a series of statements to actively involve students in making predictions about what they will be reading. To make predictions, students rely on their prior knowledge.

The teacher identifies ideas from text that may challenge or support student beliefs about the material contained in the text. An organizer of three to ten statements is created to spark student knowledge or beliefs about what they will soon read.

Before Reading

Students read the statements on the organizer and, using their prior knowledge, mark whether the statements are true or false. Responses (if desired) can be shared as a prereading discussion.

During Reading

Students read to clarify or verify predictions, noting new information.

After Reading

Students will return to the organizer and respond to the statements again. Have students discuss any changes that occur in their "before" and "after" responses.

Anticipation Guide

Social Science

Directions: Before reading, place a mark under "likely" if you feel that the statement has any truth. Put a mark under "unlikely" if you feel that it has no truth. Be ready to explain your choices.

Before Reading		Statements about Text	After Reading	
Likely	Unlikely		True	False
_____	__✓__	1. Popular sovereignty is guaranteed in the Constitution and means that some people are more popular than others.	_____	_____
__✓__	_____	2. The system of three branches of government (legislative, judicial, and executive) provides for checks and balances on each branch.	_____	_____
_____	__✓__	3. Federalism divides power between the national government and the state government.	_____	_____
_____	__✓__	4. Because of the Bill of Rights, all Americans can do what they want.	_____	_____

After reading, correct your Anticipation Guide.

Anticipation Guide

Directions: Put a mark under "likely" if you feel that the statement is true. Put a mark under "unlikely" if you feel that it has no truth. Be ready to explain your choices.

Before Reading		Statements about Text	After Reading	
Likely	**Unlikely**		**True**	**False**
_____	_____	1.	_____	_____
_____	_____	2.	_____	_____
_____	_____	3.	_____	_____
_____	_____	4.	_____	_____
_____	_____	5.	_____	_____
_____	_____	6.	_____	_____
_____	_____	7.	_____	_____
_____	_____	8.	_____	_____

After reading, correct your Anticipation Guide.

EXPLANATION FOR APPLICATION OF READING STRATEGY

Picture Walk

Before Reading

Picture Walk is from the survey section of Francis Robinson's 1946 SQ3R strategy, in which students sequentially view and discuss all pictures, charts, and drawings contained in the targeted chapter, section, or story that the class is to read. Read only picture captions and chart information. Do not read text at this time. All discussion answers or ideas are to be perceived as correct as students have not yet read the textual information. Predictions are part of the learning fun. Even though this activity is targeted for content material, it can easily be adapted to preview fictional or historical narrative. This strategy is helpful to ESL and struggling readers.

Some discussion sparkers regarding pictures, charts, and graphics may include the following:

What do you think is happening in the picture?

What do you see in the picture?

How does the picture make you feel about the character or the topic?

What does the caption have to do with the picture?

What information have you learned from the picture and caption about the topic, story, setting, or character?

What do you think the text will say about the topic or characters?

How does this picture fit in the topic and headings and/or characters and narrative?

What do the graphics or charts in the chapter tell you about the topic?

Can we create a summary sentence of what we *think* this reading will be about? (At this point students can share ideas and create their preview sentence, writing it on the following sheet.)

During Reading

Students read to clarify or verify predictions and mentally form new predictions.

After Reading

Upon completion of the reading, students fill in the reverse or bottom section of the sheet indicating the *actual* content of the material.

TEMPLATE FOR
APPLICATION OF READING STRATEGY

Picture Walk

I think this will be about . . .

_____

_____

_____

_____

_____

_____

After reading, I found out this was about . . .

_____

_____

_____

_____

_____

_____

_____

Heading through a Picture Walk

The Struggle Over the South's Future

How did the nation move toward reunion after the Civil War?

Directions: Take a picture and caption walk through the chapter. Note the pictures, headings, charts, and so forth. Use that information and what you already know on the topic to write under each topic heading.

The Defeated South
Needed rebuilding

The Freedmen
They had a lot to learn

President Johnson's Plan
Reconstruction
States govern their citizens
Confederate leaders gain power
South to reject the 14th Amendment

Johnson vs. Congress
Civil rights upheld
Congress post troops to protect slaves
Congress in control

Based on your observations and preview information, read and answer the following questions. Use pencil.

1. Define:

   Freedmen: *men who have newly gained freedom*

   Reconstruction: *rebuilding the country after the Civil War*

   Civil rights: *rights naturally given in a free society*

2. Describe Johnson's Reconstruction plan. Why did many white southerners support his plan? Why did most northerners oppose it?

   Johnson's plan left states to decide how to govern citizens. Southern states passed Black Codes. Johnson encouraged southern states not to ratify the 14th Amendment. Whites retained their power. Northerners opposed this as they believed <u>all</u> male citizens should vote.

3. How did Congress's plan differ from the president's?

   Congress passed three amendments: 13th (abolish slavery), 14th (give slaves full rights as U.S. citizens), and 15th (all male citizens have the right to vote. The president was a southerner and did not want the amendments to pass.

4. Power struggles between Congress and the president are part of the U.S. political system. What are some current conflicts between two branches of government?

   The war with Iraq.

Heading through a Picture Walk

_____

Title

Directions: Take a picture and caption walk through the chapter. Note the pictures, headings, charts, and so forth. Then, using the following headings, write down what information you think will be included in each section.

_____   _____

(Heading)   (Heading)

_____   _____

(Heading)   (Heading)

Based on your observations and preview information, read and answer the following questions. Use pencil.

1.

2.

3.

4.

EXPLANATION FOR APPLICATION OF READING STRATEGY

Think-Aloud

Think-Alouds (Davey, 1983) model the kind of strategies good readers use. It is especially effective when used to illustrate the mental steps good readers use to cope with a particular comprehension problem. The teacher needs to illustrate how she or he makes a hypothesis or prediction, pictures images, creates an analogy, monitors the comprehension, and consistently uses fix-up strategies.

Before Reading

The teacher selects a passage to read aloud that contains points of difficulty, contradictions, ambiguities, and/or unknown words. Students need to follow along silently as the teacher reads aloud. Place the text on a transparency as a visual resource for students to follow.

During Reading

Make predictions as you read aloud so that the students see how you **develop the hypotheses** about the material. *"How am I supposed to solve this problem? I need to know how many more boxes Jane has to sell to reach her goal. What do I know—her goal is 40, and she has already sold 25 boxes—I think I will find her goal by either subtracting or adding."*

Describe the picture you are forming in your head from the information. This step demonstrates how to develop images during reading. *"I have a pile of 25 boxes of school pencils on one side. Most are printed with the school name, some pencils have the school*

mascot, and there are a few boxes of plain pencils. Then I have an empty space with a question mark. Then I have an equal sign, and on the other side of the equal sign, I have a pile of 40 boxes of all kinds of school pencils."

Share an analogy by showing students how to link prior knowledge with new information in the text—the "like-a" step. *"We did a problem like this yesterday when we . . . and we did . . ."*

Talk through a confusing point to model how you monitor your ongoing comprehension. *"Do I need to add or subtract here? Let us see, I need to know what number of boxes plus what number of boxes equals 40 boxes so I must add. No, that cannot be right because 25 and 40 equals 65, and that is more than Jane's goal. I better reread. I must have to subtract the number of boxes Jane has already sold from the number of boxes that is her goal."*

Demonstrate **fix-up strategies** that may be used to clear up confusion. Model rereading, reading ahead, looking for context clues about unknown words, and any other strategies you want your students to be aware of in their reading.

After Reading

Allow students to share their reactions to the text. After several modeling experiences, have students work with partners to practice think-alouds. Encourage students to practice thinking through material on their own. Reinforce these thinking strategies with selected reading lessons and content reading.

EXPLANATION FOR APPLICATION OF READING STRATEGY

Think-Aloud with Questions

The Think-Aloud with Questions (Frank, 2001) strategy is meant to be modeled by teachers in order to share the process of "thinking" while reading. After the teacher has demonstrated repeatedly, how he or she makes a **prediction,** creates a **picture image,** forms an **analogy, monitors** comprehension, and consistently uses **fix-up** strategies, the class is ready for a classroom Think-Aloud.

Before Reading

The teacher previews the material with the class, looking at pictures, captions, headings, and questions. The teacher gives the students a copy of text containing the beginning of the selection that has been prepared with a space of about one inch between sentences.

During Reading

The teacher starts reading the passage, stopping after every sentence or two. The students then write what they are thinking on their paper underneath the appropriate sentence.

After Reading

Students then share their predictions, images, and analogies with each other and the class. They discuss how they monitor their comprehension and use fix-up strategies.

After reading the first paragraph or two in this manner, several questions are asked.

If the selection is nonfiction:

What is this about?

What information do you expect to find in the selection?

What questions will be answered in the passage?

If the selection is fiction:

Who is the main character?

What is the setting?

Are there any other important characters?

What is the main character's problem?

How do you think the main character will solve the problem?

Discussion is held as a class.

The students then read the selection, filling in a graphic organizer for nonfiction and a story map for fiction.

Think-Aloud with Questions

"Perseus"

Directions: Direct students to examine the pictures. The teacher leads a classroom Think-Aloud. During this process, the teacher reads aloud, stopping after each small section so that the teacher and the students can interpret the meaning of the passage in their own words.

Once a king named Acrisius asked a prophet about the future. The prophet said, "One day your baby grandson, Perseus, is going to kill you."

Stop and Think: How would you feel if your grandchild were about to kill you?

So Acrisius put Perseus and Perseus's mother, Danae, into a large box. He put the box into the ocean. The waves carried the box to the island of Seriphus. There Perseus grew up into a brave young man.

Stop and Think: How would you feel if you were put to sea in a box?

Now the king of Seriphus wanted to marry Danae. Perseus was against the marriage. So the king thought of a plan to get rid of Perseus. The king asked Perseus to kill a terrible monster called Medusa. The brave Perseus accepted the king's challenge.

Stop and Think: What do you think will happen now?

Questions for class discussion:

What is the name of the main character?

What are the names of the other characters?

What is the setting?

What is the main character's problem?

Note: Information from *English Yes!* by Burton Goodman, 2004, Columbus, OH: McGraw-Hill.

TEMPLATE FOR APPLICATION OF READING STRATEGY

Think-Aloud with Questions

Directions: Direct students to examine the pictures on pages _____. The teacher leads a classroom Think-Aloud. During this process, the teacher reads aloud, stopping after each small section so that the teacher and the students can interpret the meaning of the passage in their own words.

(Insert first passage)

Stop and Think:

(Insert second passage)

Stop and Think:

(Insert third passage)

Stop and Think:

Questions for class discussion:

What is the name of the main character?

What are the names of the other characters?

What is the setting?

What is the main character's problem?

EXPLANATION FOR APPLICATION OF READING STRATEGY

First, The Questions

In this prereading strategy, a modified DRTA (Stauffer, 1969), First, The Questions (Frank, 1996), highlights the teacher's role to guide students to the general and the specifics of a selection. The teacher decides what the students should know at the end of the lesson. This required information is turned into questions.

Before Reading

Students read the headings and questions. Using their prior knowledge, they answer the questions. Responses can be shared as a prereading discussion.

During Reading

Students read to clarify or verify predictions and to note new information. This can be done individually or in small groups. In their small groups, the students must reach a consensus on the exact answers to questions.

After Reading

Have students discuss any changes that occurred in their "before" and "after" responses. Share collaborative responses as a class. The teacher will record answers on an overhead or chalkboard. The class reaches consensus on specific answers. This can now be used to study for the test.

First, The Questions

Cold Facts

Directions: Each student must fill in an answer to each question. With a partner, the students come to a consensus on the predicted answers. As a class, the answers are stated and put on the board or overhead. The students read to verify, correct, or modify their answers.

1. What causes the common cold?

    A virus
    Dirty hands
    Sneezing
    Going outside with wet hair
    Not getting enough rest

2. Why should cold sufferers stop using nasal sprays or drops after three days?

    They are addicting.
    They don't work any more.

3. Why is a vaccine helpful in preventing the flu but not a cold?

    A vaccine is aimed at a specific germ.

4. What are three ways to avoid getting a cold?

    Wash your hands often.
    Dress warmly.
    Stay away from sick friends.

Note: Information from "The Cold Facts," 1998, *The Contemporary Reader, 2, #5.*

First, The Questions

(Title of Selection)

Directions: Each student must fill in an answer to each question. With a partner, the students come to a consensus on the specific answers. As a class, the answers are stated and put on the board or overhead. The students read to verify, correct, or modify their answers.

1.

2.

3.

4.

CHAPTER THREE

Instructional Frames

Instructional Frames Strategies

Curiosity and Background
Prediction Pairs
Concept Diagram
THIEVES

Engagement
Story Map
Proposition/Support
4 ■ Reciprocal Teaching
Two-Column Notes

Applications
Pyramid Frame

Instructional frames are personal road maps used for constructing meaning of content materials (Vacca & Vacca, 2005). Teachers use instructional frameworks as planning guides, whereas students use them as learning tools. The framework is used to teach the reading process (strategies) as well as the content of the reading (product) (Tierney, Readence, & Dishner, 1980).

Research Preview
Current research indicates that if the students have a learning guide to use before, during, and after reading then the construction of meaning from content materials will occur (Vacca & Vacca, 2005). Before reading, teachers need to elicit and build background knowledge (Rumelhart, 1980). During reading, teachers use graphic organizers and

various notetaking techniques that improve student comprehension of text (Clarke, 1991; Berkowitz, 1986; Piccolo, 1987). After reading, clarification and application of concepts occurs through talking, drawing, writing, and drama (Herber, 1970).

English Language Arts Standard

Reading is essential. Using strategies for constructing meaning before, during, and after reading will help students connect what they read now with what they have learned from the past. Students who read well and widely build a strong foundation for learning in all areas of life (Illinois State Board of Education, 1997).

Connections to Research

Herber (1970) created a model to describe an instructional framework. He explained the three-step instructional sequence and the rational related to each step. In prereading, the purpose is to activate prior knowledge, build motivation, and provide direction. During reading, the intent is to develop interactions with reader and text in order to provide active engagement. Postreading is used to extend, clarify, and elaborate ideas from the text. Instructional frames serve as road maps for students "to guide them in learning the ideas, concepts, and skills of a content area and in successfully using them" (Vacca & Vacca, 1996).

There are three principles of learning upon which the instructional framework is based. The first premise is that learning is based on prior understandings of the content and organization and that all new learning builds from previous experience. The second aspect is that learning involves commitment and involvement through various note-taking strategies. Finally, the third component of learning is thoughtful reflection and application. To further describe these three principles, Irwin stated:

> Proficient learners build on and activate their background knowledge before reading, writing, speaking or listening; poor learners begin without thinking. Proficient learners know their purpose for learning, give it their complete attention, and keep a constant check on their understanding; poor learners do not know or even consider whether or not they understand. Proficient learners also decide whether they have achieved their goal, and summarize and evaluate their thinking. (Irwin et al., 1995, p. 5)

It is essential that teachers provide instructional frames in order for all students to learn.

Teachers need to know three components of an instructional framework. First, they must understand the concept of *initiating*. This phase sets the stage for learning or provides the initial preparation. Generally teachers and students are engaged in the following processes during this stage (Vacca & Vacca, 1996):

Teachers do the following:

- Introduce the content.
- Assess prior knowledge.
- Spark/develop prior knowledge.
- Identify purposes and parameters.
- Plan by building on prior knowledge.
- Stimulate curiosity.
- Create a need to know.
- Develop a strategic plan for teaching.

Students do the following:

- Preview the content.
- Assess prior knowledge.
- Activate/build prior knowledge.
- Determine purposes.
- Connect with prior knowledge.
- Raise questions and issues.

- Recognize a need to know.
- Develop a strategic plan for learning.

Initiating is the first phase of the instructional process. Prior knowledge is based on schema theory, which states that students need a bridge for linking old information to new (Anderson & Pearson, 1984). It provides the initial road map that teachers will follow as they begin their journey by helping students organize, understand, and use new information. Assessing students' prior knowledge and making appropriate teacher decisions on what other information needs to be presented can have a strong influence on the success or failure of their learning experiences.

Constructing is the second phase of the instructional framework in which new understandings, skills, and knowledge are developed through active engagement by teachers and students. The strategies that teachers use include modeling, demonstrating, explaining, clarifying, elaborating, thinking aloud, sequencing, structuring, giving analogies, and creating examples. Students learn to be active participants as they think about what they have previously learned and connect it to the new material they encounter. During this phase, students need many opportunities to construct meaning from different information sources. They might react, discuss, write, and think about their own reactions and those of others. Thinking about their own thinking process (metacognition), which is done during reading and note taking, allows students to recognize how they learn. When they are able to apply this reflective process to new circumstances, the learning is more comprehensible (Vacca & Vacca, 1996).

The third phase of the instructional framework is *application*. The teacher sets the parameters for learning, but the student is responsible for using their own knowledge in this learning process. They may synthe-size, apply, problem solve, and create while they are reading. According to Graves and Graves (1994), as students think or see things in new ways, they may create or extend their ideas. This process relates to student writing as well as reading in that they begin to creatively communicate their thoughts and feelings to others.

By using an instructional framework with content material, the teacher helps students to become independent learners and thinkers. Students integrate these three phases to accomplish different tasks in the reading process. They may predict the new learning experience during the initiation phase. During construction, they predict the established relationships among the ideas presented. Finally in application, they use predictions to extend new ideas in their learning.

These strategies can be tied to content areas such as math, science, and social science as well as language arts. Examples of the following strategies and their relationship to various content areas provide the scaffolding necessary for instruction.

Prediction Pairs (Stauffer, 1969) present a reading strategy that can be incorporated in any content area. The student is guided into predicting what will happen in the text that they are reading for science, social science, or language arts. They may develop a question that they want to have answered as they read a section of text. They write the question or prediction that they propose. Then they repeat the process of questioning and responding to text through these Prediction Pairs.

Concept Diagrams (Frank, 1999) are used to highlight understandings associated with language arts, art, music, science, social science, and math. The teacher writes the concept that the students will study in a diagram on the overhead or chalkboard. As the students study the headings and visuals from the text selection, they add information that they want to address in their reading to the diagram. They may consider key words and ideas as well as pictures or examples of the concept. After reading, the students complete the diagram of the concept and share what they learned with a partner. This is later used to write a summary of the concept for use during class discussion.

THIEVES stands for the following: Title, Headings, Introduction, Every first sentence in a paragraph, Visuals and vocabulary, End-of-chapter questions, and Summary reading (Manz, 2002). This reading strategy allows students to preview the text information before reading and to establish a purpose for their reading. They are able to use the author's content and structure in order to improve their comprehension of text. This process of previewing text materials can be used in language arts, math, science, social studies, foreign language, fine arts, and physical education.

Story Maps (Beck & McKowen, 1981) are graphic organizers that are appropriately used with narrative text. The teacher previews and discusses the story elements—such as characters, setting, problem, events, and conclusion—that the students will encounter in their reading. While reading, the students respond to the sections of the Story Map that are addressed prior to reading. After reading, they discuss the written information used to address each section of the Story Map. Vocabulary that is important to understanding the story may also be addressed. This serves as a summary of the narrative text that they read.

Proposition/Support (Buehl, 2003; Cook, 1989; Santa, 1988) shows students how to organize information from reading content materials such as science, social science, math, and language arts. The students divide their paper in two columns and label the first one "Proposition" and the second one "Support." The first column presents the proposition, or statement that their reading advocates, such as "There should be more habitats for grizzly bears." The second column offers documentation as to why this proposition should be supported. Then the students draw a conclusion from their notes regarding the proposition and supporting details.

Reciprocal Teaching (Palinscar & Brown, 1984) is a dialogue process between the teacher, student, and text. It provides an opportunity for the teacher to model the following: predicting, questioning, clarifying, and summarizing. This strategy improves comprehension of text materials. It is important to note that in planning a lesson using reciprocal teaching that the predicting segment is best done as a class and the remaining segments are individual tasks.

Two-Column Notes (Palmatier, 1973) provides yet another instructional frame for understanding the content that students encounter in their reading. This note-taking strategy can be used to help students remember what they have learned in any subject area whether it be science, social studies, math, language arts, physical education, or fine arts. It can be used with text material, lectures, or films. The students capture the main idea and the important details in correct order.

The **Pyramid Frame,** taken from a Story Map, Pyramid Diagram, and Bio Poem, is useful when working with literature, especially novels (Beck & McKowen, 1981; Kinkead, Thompson, Wright, & Gutierrez, 1992; Solon, 1980). This strategy helps not only with increasing comprehension, but also with teaching visualization skills, summarizing, making inferences, or self-monitoring their reading. Before reading, the elements of the instructional frame of a Story Pyramid are reviewed. The students know what they are expected to concentrate on in their reading.

EXPLANATION FOR APPLICATION OF READING STRATEGY

Prediction Pairs

This instructional frame (Stauffer, 1969) teaches students how to support a prediction with evidence from the text. This format helps students with their thinking, writing, and classroom discussion before, during, and after reading. Students must rely on what they know through experience and their studies up to this point in making educated guesses about the text they are about to read.

Teacher and students preview the section for reading. Survey subtitles, pictures, and captions as well as end questions. Using this information as a guide, ask students to predict what will happen next by filling in the boxes in the first column. In the second column of boxes, students read and then record reasons for their predictions or correct answers.

Before Reading

Sequentially view and discuss all pictures, charts, and drawings contained in the targeted chapter, section, or story that the class is to study. The students then predict "What will happen next?" and record their thoughts in the first column.

During Reading

Students read and record facts that support their prediction in the second column of boxes.

After Reading

Upon completion of the reading, students review their predictions and responses from reading, making any corrections necessary. Answer and discuss any end questions that posed a problem for students.

Prediction Pairs

What Will Happen Next?	Reasons from Reading
(What will be included in this section?)	
1. *It will tell what Lincoln was doing when he was shot.*	*Watching a play at the Ford Theater*

What Will Happen Next?	Reasons from Reading
(What will be included in this section?)	
2. *It will tell who killed Lincoln.*	*John Wilkes Booth*

What Will Happen Next?	Reasons from Reading
(What will be included in this section?)	
3. *It will tell why Charles Giuteau was angry with President Garfield.*	*He felt he had the skills to have a government job, but Garfield refused to see him.*

What Will Happen Next?	Reasons from Reading
(What will be included in this section?)	
4. *It will tell what most Americans thought about President McKinley.*	*The American people were fond of McKinley because he was a kind and happy man.*

Prediction Pairs

What Will Happen Next?	Reasons from Reading
What Will Happen Next?	Reasons from Reading
What Will Happen Next?	Reasons from Reading
What Will Happen Next?	Reasons from Reading

EXPLANATION FOR APPLICATION OF READING STRATEGY

Concept Diagram

A Concept Diagram (Frank, 1999) provides a format for the purpose of activating prior knowledge and previewing text material. This strategy helps students understand metacognitively what is known and not known as well as the fact that text can be employed to help find information while helping the brain to store new facts.

Before Reading

On a blank transparency, write the topic about which students will be reading. Students volunteer information associated with the topic. Students are asked to examine headings, subheadings, and visuals in the text selection and gather further infor-mation. Add new information to the graphic organizer on the transparency.

During Reading

Students are asked to read the text selection carefully to support further discussion and find other relevant information or key terms that can be added to the Concept Diagram.

After Reading

Upon completion of the reading, students will complete a diagram of the concept. Partners can share their diagrams, explain what they learned, and write a summary of the basic concepts.

Concept Diagram

Concept: Art: American Romanticism	State concept in your own words: American painters began to use nature and landscapes in a more favorable way. Nature was full of wonder and the common man a hero.
Key words and ideas: Landscapes Common man Rose-colored glasses Nature Wilderness	Examples or pictures of the concept:

Describe your picture or example of the concept:

Common people making a life for themselves by using nature as they live in the wilderness of the Grand Tetons.

Note: Information from *The Annotated Mona Lisa* (p. 83) by Carol Strickland and John Boswell, 1995, Kansas City: Universal Press.

Concept Diagram

Concept:	State concept in your own words:
Key words and ideas:	**Examples or pictures of the concept:**

Describe your picture or example of the concept:

THIEVES

THIEVES (Manz, 2002) is an acronym for an individualized or group instructional frame. The acronym THIEVES stands for the elements of a complete preview of nonfiction text that allows the reader to access prior knowledge, set a purpose, and use the author's content and structure to enhance comprehension. The goal of the classroom teacher is to create enough practice with this strategy that students use it independently to increase their comprehension of difficult text.

Before Reading

This organized preview of text begins by reading the following:

T **Title and questioning:** What do I already know about this topic? What does it have to do with the preceding chapter? Does it present a point of view?

H **Headings,** the bold print outline of the subject area, are the next items to be previewed. By turning each heading into a question, the reader's thoughts are focused for the text material.

I **Introductions** are read, providing background and a general outline for the text.

E **Every first sentence in a paragraph** is read, giving a complete preview. These topic sentences usually state the main idea of the information being presented.

V **Visuals and vocabulary** are a key to a concept. Putting words to *pictures, graphs, and captions* helps students learn about a topic before the actual act of reading. In addition, recognizing the bold print vocabulary words and integrating them into the context of the chapter allows readers to express their understanding of the material in a succinct manner.

E **End-of-chapter questions** direct the reader to important information and concepts. Questions enable the student to actually learn the author's point of view and glean new information. These questions point the reader to the notes they need to take during the act of reading.

S **Summary reading** gives the students a general frame of reference along with a listing of the important details. It provides a clear knowledge structure of the details that are present in the text.

Students fill in the graphic organizer as a preview of the text.

During Reading

During the reading of the nonfiction text, the students add detailed notes to the graphic organizer. This provides each of them with a personal storage file of the needed information.

After Reading

After reading, the students reread their notes and write a more detailed summary of the information. For science or physical education, readers can make their own graphical materials. In math, students can create their own word problems, including directions. Either an expanded summary or an application of the information will guarantee comprehension and memory of the assigned text.

THIEVES

T. **Title** *Before the Mayflower*

H. **Headings**

1. *The First Blacks in America*
2. *The First Black Immigrants*
3. *The Growth of Negro Slavery*
4. *Who Were the Black Slaves in America?*

I. **Introduction**

Blacks first came to America with Spanish and Portuguese explorers. Some immigrated to Virginia as settlers, and later they were made slaves after being captured by Africans and Europeans.

E. **Every First Sentence in a Paragraph**

V. **Visuals and Vocabulary**

1. *The First Blacks in America*
   Heading
   A. *Black Christians born in Spain and Portugal were among the first settlers of the Americas.*
      Ideas from the first sentence
      1. *Blacks working on sugar plantations in South America*
         Concept from a visual
      2. *Importation*
         Vocabulary word highlighted in this subsection
2. *The First Black Immigrants*
   Heading
   A. *A million Black immigrants came to the United States because of duress and pressure.*
      Ideas from the first sentence
      1. *Poor white and black men selling their services for money.*
         Concept from a visual
      2. *Indentured servitude*
         Vocabulary word highlighted in this subsection
3. *The Growth of Negro Slavery*
   Heading
   A. *Rulers of the American colonies enslaved Blacks because of their strength.*

Ideas from the first sentence
   1. *Black men and women as slaves working in the fields.*
      Concept from a visual
   2. *Intermarriage*
      Vocabulary word highlighted in this subsection
4. *Who Were the Black Slaves in America?*
   Heading
   A. *Most Black slaves came from the West Coast of Africa.*
      Ideas from the first sentence
      1. *Black slaves being captured in African native wars and sold by African merchants to Europeans.*
         Concept from a visual
      2. *Slattees*
         Vocabulary word highlighted in this subsection

E. **End Questions**

Information learned from the questions

Blacks came with the first explorers of the New World. They were some of the first settlers and did not experience racial inferiority. Later Blacks became slaves because they could not blend into the white population. Millions were sold into slavery by Africans and Europeans.

S. **Summary**

A sentence summary of the major concept and the key supporting details.

Before the Mayflower, Blacks came to the New World with explorers to South and Central America and as settlers in Virginia. Blacks became slaves because Native Americans got sick and died and Whites could escape and blend into the population, but Blacks could not blend into the population and they were strong. Africans and Europeans were involved in the slave trade, but there were some African leaders who forbade their subjects to take part in it.

THIEVES

T. Title _____

H. Headings

1. _____   2. _____

3. _____   4. _____

I. Introduction

E. Every First Sentence in a Paragraph

V. Visuals and Vocabulary

1. _____

  Heading
  A. _____

    Ideas from the first sentence
    1. Concept from a visual
    2. Vocabulary word highlighted in this subsection

2. _____

  Heading
  A. _____

    Ideas from the first sentence
    1. Concept from a visual
    2. Vocabulary word highlighted in this subsection

3. _____

  Heading
  A. _____

    Ideas from the first sentence
    1. Concept from a visual
    2. Vocabulary word highlighted in this subsection

4. _____

  Heading
  A. _____

    Ideas from the first sentence
    1. Concept from a visual
    2. Vocabulary word highlighted in this subsection

E. End Questions

  Information learned from the questions

S. Summary

  A sentence summary of the major concept and the key supporting details

EXPLANATION FOR APPLICATION OF READING STRATEGY

Story Map

Story Maps (Beck & McKowen, 1981; Richek et al., 2002) are best used on narrative text. Students learn to focus on the parts of a story and how they fit together. Sometimes the teacher may want students to use the information found in the Story Map to write a brief summary of the story. Another valuable use for a story map organizer is as a prewriting tool for a narrative, fiction, creative writing, or math story problem. We have included several examples with varying levels of difficulty for use with literature, narratives, or summaries, or as a creative writing tool.

Before Reading

Preview and discuss story elements included on the graphic organizer to become familiar with information expectations.

During Reading

As students read the text, they identify elements of the organizer: characters, setting, problems/events, and solutions/ending as well as noting challenging vocabulary for later discussion.

After Reading

Teacher leads students as they discuss and collaborate on the elements of the organizer. From the Story Map, the students prepare a summary or generate questions regarding the narrative. Example questions follow on the next page. Discuss vocabulary that students did not understand or found challenging. Check glossary to confirm discussed word impressions.

Story Map Discussion Suggestions

Beginning of Story Questions

Character: Who is the main character? What is _____ like? Are there other significant characters?

Setting: Where does the story take place? When does the story take place?

Problem: What is _____'s problem? What does _____ need? Why is _____ in trouble?

Middle of Story Questions

Goal: What does _____ decide to do? What does _____ have to attempt to do?

Attempts or outcome: What does _____ do about _____? What happens to _____? What will _____ do now?

End of Story Questions

Resolution: How has _____ solved the problem? How has _____ achieved the goal? What would you do to solve _____'s problem?

Reaction: How does _____ feel about the problem? Why does _____ do _____? How does _____ feel about this at the end?

Theme: What is the moral of the story? What did you learn from the story? What is the major point of the story? What does this story say about _____?

Source: From R. T. Vacca & J. L. Vacca, *Content Area Reading: Literacy and Learning across the Curriculum,* 8e. Published by Allyn and Bacon, Boston, MA. Copyright © 2005 by Pearson Education. Reprinted by permission of the publisher.

Story Map

Math Example

Fraction Cafe

1/6 of a pizza	$1.85	1/8 of a blueberry pie	$1.60
1/4 of a tamale pie	$2.25	1/5 of a carrot cake	$2.10

The four Truman children went to the Fraction Cafe and ordered the same things. They each had 1/6 of a pizza and 1/5 of a carrot cake. How much did they spend altogether?

Characters: Who is the problem about?

The four Truman children

Setting: Where are the characters?

The four children have dinner at the Fraction cafe

The Problem: What you think is being asked of you?

Trying to get the cost of dinner for the four Truman children

---

Events: What are the steps involved in the problem?

1. Each child ordered

   1/6 of a pizza

   1/5 of a carrot cake

2. Four children means I need to find 4 times the cost of 1/6 of a pizza.

3. Four children means I need to find 4 times the cost of 1/5 of a carrot cake.

4. The answers need to be added to get the total cost of the dinner.

Resolution: How did you solve the problem?

4 times 1/6 or 4 x $1.85 = $7.40

4 times 1/5 or 4 x $2.10 = $8.40

ADD $7.40

     + 8.40

     $15.80 is the total that the four Truman children spent on dinner.

Story Map

Math

Insert Problem:

Characters: Who is the problem about?

Setting: Where are the characters?

The Problem: What you think is being asked of you?

Events: What are the steps involved in the problem?

1.

2.

3.

4.

Resolution: How did you solve the problem?

Story Map

Pandora's Box

A Greek Myth

Characters:

1. *Pandora*   2. *Epimetheus*   3.

Setting:

Time: *Ancient Times*

Place: *Greece*

Goal of Main Character(s)	**Main Character's Problem**
Pandora wants to look in the box.	*She is forbidden to open the box.*

Events

1. *Pandora was sent to live with Epimetheus.*

2. *Pandoras curiosity about the box*

3. *Pandora releasing all the Troubles*

4. *Pandora and Epimetheus releasing Hope*

The conclusion or resolution was

Hope was placed in the bottom of the box so that Troubles would not seem so bad.

The lesson learned was

As long as people have Hope, they cannot always be unhappy.

Story Map

_____   _____
Title   Author

Characters:

1.   2.   3.

The Setting:

Time:
Place:

Goal of Main Character(s)	**Main Character's Problem**

Events

The conclusion or resolution was

The lesson learned was

EXPLANATION FOR APPLICATION OF READING STRATEGY

Proposition and Support

Proposition and Support (Buehl, 2003; Cook, 1989; Santa et al., 2004) is an organizational outline that teaches students how to support an argument with evidence. Students find the format useful for organizing information from reading assignments and for prewriting activities. Students can use this outline format before, during, or after reading. It provides structures that help students organize their thinking, writing, and classroom discussions.

Before Reading

The students divide their paper into two columns and label the columns "Proposition" and "Support." The teacher does the same on the board. The teacher models a proposition about the text they will be reading and puts that statement in the "Proposition" column.

During Reading

The students read the selection, locating and recording evidence from the text. The sup-

porting details are added to the "Support" column.

After Reading

After reading, the students can rethink the proposition and find appropriate evidence in the selection to support it. Next, the teacher guides the students as they construct a summary paragraph based on the proposition statement and the details that support it. The students use the following questions as a checklist for analyzing their summaries:

Is my statement clear?

Do I need more evidence to support my statement?

Is my most convincing fact placed in a position in this paragraph where it stands out clearly?

Could I move facts around in a way that would make my ideas clearer to the reader?

Proposition and Support

Proposition:	Support:
There should be more habitat for grizzly bears.	Grizzly bears are a threatened species. Problem caused by hunters, people encroaching on habitat. Logging operations decrease grizzly habitat in Forest Service lands. Hiking, camping, and hunting activities interfere with grizzlies.
Conclusion:	Human activities interfere with grizzly bears and limitations may need to be placed on human activities within the grizzly habitat.

Proposition and Support

Proposition:	Support:
Conclusion:	

4 ■ Reciprocal Teaching

Reciprocal Teaching (Palincsar & Brown, 1984) and Four Square Reciprocal Teaching (Frank, 2004) are interactive dialogues between the teacher and students regarding segments of text. The dialogues involve four strategies: predicting, question generating, clarifying, and summarizing. The prediction part of the process is done after a picture walk, a check of the end questions, and a reading of the first and last paragraphs of the passage. The students fill in the square on their reciprocal teaching sheet based on what they predict will occur in the text. Next, the teacher reads a passage and demonstrates the four strategies, the students take turns assuming the role of discussion leader. Once the students understand the process, they are put into cooperative groups where each person reads one section of the text and reports back to the group on the clarification of difficult words and concepts, with questions, and with a summary.

Before Reading

The students and the teacher take a picture walk through the text, examine the end questions, and read the first and last paragraphs.

The students discuss and then write in the square marked "Predicting" what information will be given in the text.

The teacher divides the class into groups based on the length of the reading assignment. Each student is assigned to read one section of the text.

During Reading

Each student reads his or her section of text silently and prepares the information for the other three sections on the instructional frame: a question, a clarification of a difficult concept or word, and a summary.

After Reading

After reading, students take turns assuming the role of discussion leader. While the discussion leader covers the assigned material, the other students add to the discussion by clarifying vocabulary or concepts, answering the question, and commenting on the summary.

4 ■ Reciprocal Teaching

1. Look at the picture of the scuba diver and read the first and last paragraph aloud to the class.
   a. The main idea of the first paragraph: A scuba diver must know and be able to do many things.
   b. The main idea of the last paragraph: Once trained, a scuba diver can go into any kind of water.
2. Ask the class what scuba diving information will be covered in paragraphs 2, 3, 4, and 5.
3. The students respond aloud and then record their predictions in the square marked "Predicting" on their strategy sheets.
4. Groups of four are created. Each student is assigned one of the four paragraphs.
5. The students silently read their assigned paragraph and fill in the squares marked, "Questioning," "Clarifying," and "Summarizing."
6. After reading, students take turns as discussion leader for their section.

Discussion Leader _____ Paragraph 2

Predicting	**Clarifying**
This article will tell me about scuba diving equipment and how to train to be a scuba diver.	*Scuba means self-contained underwater breathing apparatus.*
Questioning	**Summarizing**
Why would someone want to scuba dive instead of snorkel? *Because if you only snorkel you cannot stay underwater longer than you can hold your breath.*	*The author wants you to know that the term "scuba" means self-contained underwater breathing apparatus and that with this equipment you can stay underwater for an hour and go one hundred feet below the surface of the water.*

Discussion Leader _____ Paragraph 3

Predicting	**Clarifying**
This article will tell me about scuba diving equipment and how to train to be a scuba diver.	*The equipment is very specialized. The key element is the breathing device.*
Questioning	**Summarizing**
What does the breathing device look like? How does it work?	*The equipment needed for scuba diving is: a face mask, a set of fins, a rubber suit and gloves, a weight belt, a safety vest, an air tank, a special breathing device, a special diving flag and float.*

4 ■ Reciprocal Teaching-1

Predicting

What is your prediction for this passage?

What strategies will you use to help your group predict?

Clarifying

What words, phrases, or ideas do you or members of your group need clarified?

Questioning

What "quality questions" are you going to ask your group?

1.

2.

3.

Summarizing

Write your summary for this passage. Focus on "What does the author want me to know?" or "What is this about?"

4 ■ Reciprocal Teaching-2

Predicting
Predict what is likely to come next.

Clarifying Concepts and Vocabulary
Clear up the confusing parts. Find something that was confusing to you or that might be hard for younger students to understand. Then reread, analyze unknown words, look at illustrations, charts, and so on to clarify.

Questioning
Ask a question about what you read. Give the rest of the group time to respond.

Summarizing
Read the section of the text, then summarize.

Topic

What is in the beginning?	What is in the middle?	What is at the end?

What does the author want you to know, think, feel, or do?

Two-Column Notes

(Cornell Notes)

Two-Column Notes (Palmatier, 1973) can be used with all content area material, lectures, movies, or textbooks. Begin by duplicating the template that follows or by folding a sheet of notebook paper into a narrow and wide column lengthwise. This format will allow students to note main ideas and important details in an orderly manner. As with all the strategies, placing an example on a transparency and using an overhead projector to demonstrate your thinking while working through the example will help students be successful in using the Two-Column Notes.

Before Reading

Look at the titles, subtitles, bold print words, pictures, maps, captions, and questions. The teacher and students will determine the main idea from each title or subtitle and list the main idea in the narrow (left) column.

During Reading

Students are asked to read the text selection carefully and to take notes that support the main idea in the wide column (right side). Be sure to record key words and phrases, and to draw pictures or diagrams as needed. Stay away from copying complete sentences.

After Reading

Upon completion of the reading, students will compose a sentence or two for each subheading using the subheading as well as the notes to create a complete thought. Discuss as a class or in small groups to verify the students' understanding of the notes and conclusions drawn.

Two-Column Notes

Search for the Northwest Passage	
English Exploration	1. John Cabot 2. 1497—Newfoundland
French Exploration	1. Giovanni do Verrazano 2. Jacques Cartier 3. 1534—St. Lawrence River 4. Samuel de Champlain 5. 1603—St. Lawrence River settlement
Dutch Exploration	1. Henry Hudson 2. 1609—Hudson River

Two-Column Notes

Two-Column Notes

EXPLANATION FOR APPLICATION OF READING STRATEGY

Pyramid Frame

The Pyramid Frame (Beck & McKowen, 1981; Kinkead, Thompson, Wright, & Gutier-rez, 1992; Solon, 1980; Richek et al., 2002) strategy gives students opportunities to apply comprehension strategies for construction of meaning as well as teaching visualization skills, summarizing, drawing inferences, making connections, and self-monitoring reading.

Prepare an overhead transparency of this instructional frame. Demonstrate the process of completing the Pyramid Frame and use the information to organize a summary of the literary selection.

Before Reading

Review the elements required on the Pyramid Frame.

During Reading

Students are asked to read the text selection/novel, keeping in mind the elements for the Pyramid Frame.

After Reading

Upon completion of the reading, students will complete the Pyramid Frame individually or in pairs using information from the text to correctly identify the requested literary elements. Students may collaborate on answers and share as a class. The teacher may request students to write a summary of the Pyramid Frame data.

Alternative Directions for a Narrative

1. One word describing the main character
2. Two words describing the setting (time, place)
3. Three words telling about the problem
4. Four words telling about the solution
5. Five words stating a question you would like to have asked the author

1. Name of main character
2. Two words describing main character
3. Three words describing setting
4. Four words stating problem
5. Five words describing first event
6. Six words describing second event
7. Seven words describing third event
8. Eight words stating solution

1. One word identifying the main topic or content of today's lesson
2. Two interesting words from the reading
3. Three words representing the main topic of study
4. Four words representing reasons this is important today
5. Five words that summarize the section
6. Six words stating a question you would like to ask

Be sure to substitute your own questions if necessary in order to serve the purpose of the literary task. Substitute other alternative directions in order to use the Pyramid Frame to support science or social studies.

Pyramid Frame

Directions:

1. Write the theme of the literary work.

2. Write the first and last name of the main character or name a second main character.

3. Write three characteristics of the main character (adjectives).

4. Write four words that describe the setting.

5. Write five words to classify the kind of literary work that was read.

6. Using six words, write a sentence that states the problem or conflict in the literary work.

7. Using seven words, write a sentence that tells about an important event in the literary work.

8. Using eight words, write a sentence that tells about the solution to the problem or conflict in the literary work.

The Sign of the Beaver by Elizabeth George Speare

1. _Responsibility_

2. _Matt   Attean_

3. _Dependable responsible loyal_

4. _Maine wilderness cabin 1700s_

5. _A realistic historical fiction novel_

6. _Matt struggles to survive without help_

7. _Matt refuses to go with Attean's people_

8. _Matt remains and his family finally arrives safely_

Summary: _The theme of this historical fiction novel is responsibility. The main character is Matt, who shows he is dependable, responsible, and loyal at thirteen. Matt is left alone in the Maine wilderness to care for the family cabin. A nearby family of Native Americans give support to the young man. Attean, son of a Native American, teaches Matt about survival in the woods. The tribe leaves the area and invites Matt to travel with them. Matt chooses to await his family and many months later they return. Matt's responsible behavior shows he has indeed become a man._

Note: From The Sign of the Beaver by Elizabeth George Speare. New York: Dell Publishing.

Pyramid Frame

Directions:

1. _____

2. _____ _____

3. _____ _____ _____

4. _____ _____ _____ _____

5. _____ _____ _____ _____ _____

6. _____ _____ _____ _____ _____ _____

7. _____ _____ _____ _____ _____ _____ _____

8. _____ _____ _____ _____ _____ _____ _____ _____

Summary (write from Pyramid Frame ideas):

CHAPTER FOUR

Vocabulary

Vocabulary Strategies

Background Knowledge

Partner Knowledge Rater+
RIVET
Possible Sentences

Engaging and Extending

List-Group-Label
Concept Circles
Frayer Model
Cloze Procedure
Magic Squares
Magnet Summaries

Connections

Word Map
Semantic Feature Analysis

Words have many meanings that students begin to decipher through incidental and environmental learning as well as through wide reading, listening, and discussion (Blachowicz & Fisher, 2002). Most students learn from 3,000 to 4,000 words per year (Nagy & Anderson, 1984; Nagy & Herman, 1987). Teachers provide many strategies that increase word knowledge and increase student understanding of content reading materials.

Research Preview

Current research indicates that there is a strong connection between the vocabulary knowledge one possesses with their ability to comprehend what is read (Davis, 1968;

National Reading Panel, 2000). Vocabulary learning moves on a continuum of not knowing the meaning of a word to understanding its meaning to gaining a deeper more flexible knowledge of the word that allows students to encounter and use words easily during communication (Carey, 1978; Dale, 1965; McKeown & Beck, 1989; Stahl, 1985).

English Language Arts Standard

Students adjust their use of spoken, written, and visual language (e.g., conventions, style, vocabulary) to communicate effectively with a variety of audiences and for different purposes. Students use their knowledge of word meaning and their word identification strategies to comprehend, interpret, evaluate, and appreciate texts. (NCTE and IRA, 1996)

Connections to Research

Research has clearly indicated for quite some time that students' reading ability is affected by their vocabulary knowledge (Whipple, 1925). This is especially true with respect to reading content materials. If students do not grasp the meaning of words presented in text, then their understanding of that material will definitely be hindered. Teachers need to provide strategies that help students understand the vocabulary so that they can comprehend what they read.

According to research, as outlined in *Put Reading First,* four types of vocabulary need to be emphasized (Armbruster & Osborn, 2001). These include the following:

- Listening vocabulary—understanding the words that we hear
- Speaking vocabulary—knowing what words to use when we speak
- Reading vocabulary—knowing words to understand what we read
- Writing vocabulary—using appropriate words when we write

According to a review of the research on vocabulary instruction conducted by the National Reading Panel (2000), vocabulary needs to be taught both formally (directly) and informally (indirectly). Providing multiple exposures to vocabulary will assist with remembrance and understanding of the word or multiple meanings associated with it. Direct instruction should engage students in activities that will help them in understanding the vocabulary in order to strengthen their comprehension of text. This can be accomplished through the application of several key concept-building strategies related to enhancing vocabulary. Additional ways that teachers can assist students with word acquisition include electronic text, incidental learning, use of enriched contexts, and exposure to wide and varied reading.

When reading narrative materials, the context or a student's prior knowledge can often suffice. It is much more important to teach vocabulary when students engage in learning new concepts or encounter new terminology particularly in content areas such as science, social science, fine arts, and math. Their ability to use the vocabulary and comprehend its meaning is increased when teachers concentrate on preteaching vocabulary and the development of concepts (Beck et al., 1982; Mezynski, 1983; Stahl & Fairbanks, 1986).

Regarding vocabulary instruction, research provides seven suggestions that a teacher should use simultaneously (Blachowicz & Fisher, 2002):

- Vocabulary learning takes place when students are immersed in words.
- Vocabulary learning takes place when students are active in discovering how words are related to experiences and to one another.
- Vocabulary learning takes place when students personalize word learning.
- Vocabulary learning builds on multiple sources of information.

- Vocabulary learning takes place when students control their own learning.
- Vocabulary learning takes place when students are aided in developing independent strategies.
- Vocabulary learning is long lasting when students use words in meaningful ways.

This information is helpful in planning instructional strategies that will assist students with learning vocabulary and thereby increasing their comprehension.

The more that the teacher plans to incorporate before, during, and after reading strategies that structure learning related to vocabulary acquisition and concept attainment, the more likely students will develop deep understandings of content materials (Anderson & Pearson, 1984). It is always important to determine what students know about words by activating their prior knowledge. This can cement learning for those who have specific understandings related to the content to be studied, while at the same time building background for those students who do not have a great deal of background knowledge. These activities can help students make connections between what they know and what they read. In fact, during reading, the students build knowledge by constructing meaning from the text. They clarify understandings through vocabulary encountered in the context of their reading. After reading, the students—with assistance from the teacher—define and clarify what the words actually mean and how this helps them understand the concepts presented in the content areas. The students learn how to use these words through listening, speaking, and writing (Vacca & Vacca, 2005). The students are then more likely to understand the vocabulary when they read other materials.

It is important to remember that students can be taught to construct the meanings of words through thoughtful planning on the teacher's part. By providing frequent and varied instruction that is designed to group vocabulary into meaningful categories or schemas rather than in isolation, students can make connections in their learning (Blachowicz, 1986). The following steps are ones that teachers can use to assure that vocabulary learning does occur:

1. Activate prior knowledge.
2. Make predictive connections.
3. Encounter the words in text.
4. Refine and reformulate the word meanings.
5. Use words in writing and see words in additional reading.

These instructional steps can assist students in developing meaningful word knowledge.

According to Terman (1916) and later Sternberg (1987), one of the best indicators of verbal ability is vocabulary knowledge. Therefore, if a teacher plans instruction to increase understandings of key vocabulary in the content areas, then one aspect of a student's multiple intelligences (Gardener, 1983), namely linguistic, which influences verbal ability, is strengthened. Other areas of intelligence such as musical, logical-mathematical, spatial, bodily-kinesthetic, and personal are also strengthened through the use of vocabulary enhancement strategies.

Providing extensive opportunities for reading many different materials, not only in school but also at home, can increase students' vocabulary and comprehension as well as expand their knowledge base (Allington, 1994; Anderson, Wilson, & Fielding, 1988; Guthrie et al., 1995; Nagy & Herman, 1987). Teachers can encourage students to read and make personal interpretations of text by creating an environment that allows time for discussion. Students become more independent in their learning through wide and varied reading opportunities that require the application of strategies introduced by the teacher in the classroom. The more every teacher in a school initiates these strategies, the more likely the students will incorporate understanding and application of learning skills to other reading and contexts, such as speaking and writing.

According to Klein (1988), there are 750,000 words in the English language, but only 10,000 are used by most adults. Teachers can use many strategies to help students develop an understanding of important words as well as increase their command of English. They need not only to help students learn new vocabulary and increase their use of that vocabulary in reading and writing, but also to help them transfer its use to new situations. With increased understandings, students learn new concepts encountered in content areas such as science, social science, language arts, fine arts, and math.

One strategy that teachers can use to increase vocabulary learning in reading is called the **Knowledge Rating** (Blachowicz, 1986). The new words are listed in the first column of a chart related to a particular concept, such as weather. The students make a prediction about what the words in each row mean and write their understandings in the second column of the chart. Then they converse with a partner and collaboratively compose a new theory. This is written in the third column of the chart. Finally they read the text related to weather and then write their new ideas associated with the concept and the various vocabularies related to that concept in the final fourth column. While this example describes how to use this strategy with science, it could easily be applied to social science, math, language arts, fine arts, physical education, or health. **Partner Knowledge Rater+** is Cecilia Frank's adaptation of this format. See her examples.

A **RIVET** (Katz, 1999; Frank, 2000) is a term used to signify that the teacher has the students' attention riveted to the key vocabulary from science, social science, and language arts. The teacher uses the key vocabulary from a piece of nonfiction text and places it under a chapter's subheading. The letters in the key words are counted and slash marks (or blanks) are used instead of the words. The students use the title, the subtitle, a picture walk through the chapter, and the number of slash marks (or blanks) to predict what words are appropriate under each subheading. The teacher helps them predict the words by giving the students the word letter by letter until someone guesses the correct word. This forces the students to use their prior knowledge of the topic and the structure of the chapter to predict the key concept words. Once all the words are filled in under each heading, the students write a prereading paragraph using the title, subtitles, and the key concept words. As the students read and create their study outline, they verify or reject their predictions, along with adding key details to each subheading and concept word. When they are done with their silent reading, they rewrite their paragraphs, adding the appropriate details to the prereading paragraph.

Possible Sentences (Stahl & Kapinus, 1991; Blachowicz & Fisher, 2002) is a prereading and vocabulary activity that draws on students' prior knowledge and gets students to think of relationships between concepts. It is especially useful to work with words that are associated with a single discipline, such as science or social science. Possible sentences can be used to produce greater understanding of vocabulary and recall of text information. It provides multiple exposures to the vocabulary that teachers want students to learn as the students see the word through the sentences that have been generated, as they read the text, and in the follow-up activities. It definitely improves comprehension and learning from content area materials.

List-Group-Label (Taba, 1967; Blachowicz & Fisher, 2002) is a strategy that increases understanding of the concept through a predictive vocabulary activity.

Students brainstorm lists of words related to the concept, form learning teams to group the words into logical arrangements, and then label each arrangement. For example, if the teacher was conducting a science lesson related to animals and asked the students to name as many different animals as they could, they would brainstorm a complete list of animals and then place them in classifications related to the six animal groups: mammals, birds, reptiles, amphibians, fish, and insects. This could easily be done in math if the students were asked to name as many terms as possible. They could then label them according to specific categories such as measurement, fractions, and geometric shapes. In music, they might brainstorm all the instruments they could identify and then classify according to specific types. This increases the students' understanding of vocabulary for classifications of specific content areas.

A **Concept Circle** (Artley, 1975; Vacca & Vacca, 2005) is another way to critically reinforce study words after reading. The circle is divided into four equal sections with words or phrases assigned to each. Students are expected to identify the concept relationships that exist among the sections. One section may or may not actually contain a phrase that does not relate to the other sections. This helps to clarify understandings of the concept. Students have a visual representation to use in helping them clarify the categorization of concepts that are presented through this strategy. For example, in social science, the following words might be written in each section of the circle: socialism, democracy, political system, and anarchy. Students could give a general label to the four words and then use the words in context to compare and express understanding of their meanings. This strategy could easily be applied to science, math, fine arts, and physical education.

Another reading strategy is the **Frayer Model** (Frayer, Frederick, & Klausmeier, 1969), which helps connect what students know with what they will learn. The main concept is written in the center of the graphic organizer. A large square is divided into four smaller squares. The upper left square addresses the essential characteristics related to the concept, while the opposite upper right square deals with nonessential characteristics. The lower left square provides examples, and the lower right square shows the nonexamples. For example, if angiosperm is the main concept, the essential characteristics might include the following: produces flowers, fruit, and covered seeds. The nonessential characteristics might indicate the color of the flower, the kind of fruit, and the number of seeds. Examples of angiosperm could be peas, roses, and grass, whereas nonexamples might depict cedar, moss, or fern. By differentiating these aspects of the concept, greater categorization clarification related to vocabulary is achieved. The Frayer Model can be incorporated when working in science, social science, math, language arts, fine arts, and physical education.

A **Cloze** (Bloomer, 1962; Bluemfield & Miller, 1966; Guice, 1969) is a procedure to help students infer word meanings through the context of what they read. The teacher selects a passage from the text and omits selected words. Then the students in the class need to supply the appropriate words to create a meaningful passage. After completing the Cloze, students read the passage from the text. They then work with the class, a partner, or individually to once again complete the Cloze. This Cloze helps them to recognize key concept words in any content area. This procedure can be used with science, social science, language arts, math, fine arts, and physical education.

Magic Squares (Vacca & Vacca, 2005) is a reading activity that helps students to define vocabulary words that they are studying in text material. The students can gain greater understanding of the vocabulary through using the terms and concepts that relate to the chapter. The students use magic numbers to complete the chart with appropriate vocabulary words and review the definitions for each of the words based on the number that each word has been assigned. The activity is a fun exercise for students and helps to cement the new vocabulary and its meaning with the content that the students are studying in science, social science, math, and language arts.

Magnet Summaries (Buehl, 2003; Hayes, 1989; Vacca & Vacca, 2005) provide the opportunity for teachers to help students identify key terms or concepts from reading a selection or chapter in their science, social science, or math text. The students write ideas about the key vocabulary words on cards to help them remember aspects related to the vocabulary that they are studying. The students then collaboratively write a four or five sentence summary paragraph to highlight the most important information pertaining to these vocabulary words.

Word Maps (Schwartz & Raphael, 1985; Blachowicz & Fisher, 2002; Buehl, 2003) are graphic organizers used to increase understanding in reading science, social science, math, language arts, fine arts, and physical education material. These graphics allow readers to enhance vocabulary and build conceptual knowledge. This map helps students to visualize a definition associated with the word to determine what a concept, such as an animal, actually is in their reading. Then the students define the animal and name the category, such as dog. Next, as the students read, they provide details describing what the dog is like. They name various characteristics of the dog, such as warm blooded, four paws, hairy, and man's best friend. Finally, some examples of types of dogs such as poodle, schnauzer, dachshund, and golden retriever are listed. Students could use *Inspiration* software to create a Word Map related to specific research on a topic. These Word Maps could be displayed in the classroom to further expand students' conceptual vocabulary.

Semantic Feature Analysis (Johnson & Pearson, 1984; Blachowicz & Fisher, 2002; Buehl, 2003) could be used to clarify concepts in a specific lesson, such as geometry. The teacher would introduce a graphic organizer to help clarify concepts of specific terms. For example, the various categories might be parallelogram, rectangle, rhombus, and square. These would be the headings for the four columns. The rows would provide various descriptions of each, such as diagonals bisect each other, diagonals are congruent, each diagonal bisects a pair of opposite angles, diagonals form two pairs of congruent triangles, diagonals form four congruent triangles, and diagonals are perpendicular to each other. The students would check the appropriate box that applies to each of the geometric terms. This analysis could easily be done in any content area as students study specific concepts associated with subjects that they encounter.

All of these reading strategies can effectively be taught in any classroom. The more opportunities that a student has to use these strategies within the classroom and particularly across several content areas in many classrooms, the more likely they are to create their own graphic organizers and apply them to their own independent learning experiences.

EXPLANATION FOR APPLICATION OF READING STRATEGY

Partner Knowledge Rater+

The Knowledge Rating Strategy (Blachowicz, 1986) was redesigned by Frank (1998) and named *Partner Knowledge Rater+*. This strategy directs students, before they read, to analyze what they already know about words related to a specific topic. The students attempt a definition using words or pictures. Second, with a partner, they discuss and expand on their attempted definitions. This, too, is done before reading. As the students read, they reevaluate their predictions by confirming, modifying, or disconfirming their previously arrived at definitions. After reading, they return to the knowledge rater chart and fill in the correct content-specific definitions.

Before Reading

From the selection, the teacher chooses a list of vocabulary words that cluster in some way. These words are put on a grid where the students attempt to define and expand on their knowledge of the selected words.

The following categories are also on the grid: (1) try to define or guess the definition, (2) collaborate with a partner, (3) after reading or second try. This leads the students to make appropriate predictions about the author's use of the listed words. The students then share their predicted definitions with the class.

During Reading

The students read the selection watching for the listed vocabulary words. As they read, they confirm, disconfirm, or modify their understanding of the words.

After Reading

After reading, the students go back to the Partner Knowledge Rater+ grid and redefine the content-specific words in the third column of the matrix. These words are used in further oral or written work, such as a written paragraph.

Partner Knowledge Rater+

Weather

What Is Weather?

Directions: Predict the definitions of the following words. You may use any word you can think of, or you may draw a picture. When you are finished, share your results with your partner. Agree on a definition. After reading, decide if your definition needs further investigation. Look up the word in the dictionary if needed.

Define the Following Words	First Try Guess or Drawing	Collaborate with a Partner	After Reading or Second Try
Weather	How it feels out		Usual climate
Humidity	Makes air hotter	Moisture in air	Moisture in air
Relative Humidity	No idea . . .		Ratio air to water
Saturated	Very full	Full as can be	Very full
Dew Point	Moisture in air		Moisture in air
Fog		Low cloud	Low cloud
Precipitation	Rain		Rain
Rain Formation		Clouds	Evaporation

Partner Knowledge Rater+

_____

Title

Directions: Predict the definitions of the following words. You may use any word you can think of, or you may draw a picture. When you are finished, share your results with your partner. Agree on a definition. After reading, decide if your definition needs further investigation. Look up the word in the dictionary if needed. Now, use as many of the words as you can to write a paragraph about this topic.

Define the Following Words	First Try Guess or Drawing	Collaborate with a Partner	After Reading or Second Try

RIVET

The RIVET (Katz, 1999; Frank, 2000) strategy is designed to activate students' prior knowledge and encourage them to make vocabulary predictions before they read. Activating students' thoughts increases involvement with text and enhances comprehension for most students. To prepare for a RIVET text introduction, the teacher will read the selection and pick six to ten important words related to the concept. On the overhead, or use your chalkboard, number from 1–6 (or 10) and place a blank space for each letter of the targeted words. Another preparation task is to note text headings or categories and list them on the overhead or a student organizer. Text headings can be turned into questions to direct student note taking.

Before Reading

Under each subheading, predict the vocabulary words. Fill in letters of the first word one at a time. Students write the letters on their paper as you write them on an overhead or board. Encourage them to guess the word. Once the word is guessed, have students help spell the remainder of the word. If all agree the spelling is correct, begin the next word. The attention of students is generally "riveted" (thus, the name). If an incorrect guess is ventured, just write the next letter and have them try again. Continue until all targeted words are identified.

Now that the important vocabulary words are identified, students will write a brief paragraph using the subheadings and accompanying words. Turn headings from the text into questions and direct student note taking using the headings and the selected vocabulary words.

During Reading

Using text headings or teacher-selected categories as a guide, students take notes for each topic being sure to include vocabulary words from the RIVET.

After Reading

Students rewrite their prereading paragraph adding as many details as possible. Include a general statement and details for each of the headings or categories from the text.

RIVET

A. Prereading Vocabulary Activity

How do scientists classify animals?

<u>v e r t e b r a t e</u> <u>i n v e r t e b r a t e</u>

What are some classes of cold-blooded vertebrates?

<u>f i s h</u> <u>a m p h i b i a n</u> <u>r e p t i l e</u>

What are some classes of warm-blooded vertebrates?

<u>b i r d s</u> <u>m a m m a l s</u>

Orders of mammals

<u>m a r s u</u> __ __ __ __ __ __

__ __ __-__ __ __ __ __ __ __ __ __ __ __ __ __ __ __

__ __ __ __ __ __ __ __ __ __ __ __ __

B. During Reading: Note Taking

1. How do scientists classify animals?

   Vertebrates and invertebrates

2. What are some classes of cold-blooded vertebrates?

(Examples)	Where they live	What they look like	Examples
Fish			
Amphibians			
Reptiles			

3. What are some classes of warm-blooded vertebrates?

(Examples)	Where they live	What they look like	Examples
Birds			
Mammals			

4. Order of Mammals

(Examples)	Where they live	What they look like	Examples
Marsupials			
Sea-going			
Rodents			
Primates			

RIVET

A. Prereading Vocabulary Activity

(Insert text headings or categories, adjust blanks to fit words.)

1. __ __ __ __ __ __ __ __ __ __
   __ __ __ __ __ __ __ __ __ __ __ __

2. __ __ __ __
   __ __ __ __ __ __ __ __ __
   __ __ __ __ __ __ __ __

3. __ __ __ __ __
   __ __ __ __ __ __ __

4. __ __ __ __ __ __ __ __ __
   __ __ __ __ __ __ __ __ __ __ __ __ __
   __ __ __ __ __ __ __
   __ __ __ __ __ __ __ __

B. During Reading: Note Taking

(Turn text headings into questions to direct student note taking.)

1. (Subheading as question)

   (Student Notes)

2. (Subheading as question)

   (Student Notes)

3. (Subheading as question)

   (Student Notes)

4. (Subheading as question)

   (Student Notes)

Possible Sentences

In Possible Sentences (Stahl & Kapinus, 1991; Blachowicz & Fisher, 2002), the teacher chooses eight to ten words that may cause difficulty for their students in the targeted area of content text. The focus is on key concepts. In this strategy, students are predicting how these key vocabulary words will be used in text.

Before Reading

The teacher writes eight to ten words on the board. A brief definition may be provided. Students are directed to think of Possible Sentences that may occur in the chapter or section they are about to read. Each student or group writes a collection of sentences containing four words from the choices on the board. The goal is to use as many of the words as possible. The teacher collects the Possible Sentences.

During Reading

The students are directed to read the selection watching for the listed vocabulary words. As they read, they confirm or modify their understanding of the words.

After Reading

Following the reading, the teacher returns the Possible Sentences. The students then evaluate each sentence by placing the appropriate letters in front of each sentence:

T—true or accurate

F—false or inaccurate

M—maybe

DK—don't know

Possible Sentences

The Legendary Land

Key Terms

saga

encounter

Vikings

legendary

Leif Eriksson

exploration

cartographers

knoll

Greenlanders

geographers

Student   **Possible Sentences using terms above:**

DK   1. A saga was a time of many sad events during exploration.

F   2. A knoll is a type of knot Leif Eriksson ties.

DK   3. ET had a legendary encounter with a family in California.

F   4. Greenlanders and Vikings were geographers.

T   5. Cartographers record sagas.

M   6. Leif Eriksson was a geographer and cartographer.

T—true or accurate

F—false or inaccurate

M—maybe

DK—don't know

After reading the selection, rewrite the sentences to reflect a true statement.

Possible Sentences

_____
Title

Key Terms

1   2.   3.

4.   5.   6.

7.   8.   9.

10.   11.   12.

Possible Sentences created by students using the above terms:

_____1.

_____2.

_____3.

_____4.

_____5.

_____6.

_____7.

_____8.

T—true or accurate

F—false or inaccurate

M—maybe

DK—don't know

After reading the selection, rewrite the sentences to reflect a true statement.

EXPLANATION FOR APPLICATION OF READING STRATEGY

List-Group-Label

In the List-Group-Label strategy (Taba, 1967; Blachowicz & Fisher, 2002), brainstorming allows students to share words they know that are associated with a key concept. Students access their prior knowledge in relation to the concept the teacher has chosen for their focus. Producing lists of words helps students be aware of how much they know about the topic already and captures their interest.

An extension of this brainstorming begins once the multitude of words are listed. Using the master list from the board or overhead, group and classify the words into logical arrangements. This can be done in student teams of two to four. The teams then label each arrangement. The teacher may prefer to provide the category labels, and the teams can classify each word from the master list.

Computer connection: *Inspiration* software would be an excellent tool for students to use to show classification and categorization of words.

Before Reading

The teacher initiates a brainstorming activity on a subject students are about to encounter in text. Once the words are recorded on the board or an overhead transparency, teams of students group the words into logical arrangements. Through student discussion and debate, a label is affixed to each list.

During Reading

During reading, the students use the lists of words as a means of learning about the vocabulary while enriching the depth of their vocabulary knowledge.

After Reading

Determine if listed words are grouped with the most appropriate label. Make any changes necessary. Discuss lists, groupings, and labels as a class. Note how associations of words help with student understanding.

List-Group-Label

Students brainstorm all words they can think of related to the "Civil War."

blue	farms	guns	cannons
rebel	Lincoln	General Grant	gray
soldiers	armies	death	horses
Booth	Gettysburg Address	factories	slavery
Yankee	Ford Theater	roots	victory
assassination	slavery	plantation	freedom
General Lee	underground railroad		

Directions: Using 3 × 5 cards, each learning group will print each word on a separate card. Students will work within their learning group to classify the words in a logical category. This exercise could be completed using *Inspiration* on the computer. The individual word cards allow the students to move words between categories to see how words fit together. Students will name their final categories. Older students can organize lists of words on a sheet of paper.

Example:

North	South	Both
Yankee	rebel	armies
factories	plantation	farms
Lincoln	Lee	soldiers
victory	slavery	horses
Grant	gray	underground railroad

List-Group-Label

Brainstorm words and place on cards.

(Board/Overhead)

Categorize words and determine a label for each category.

Concept Circles

Concept Circles (Vacca & Vacca, 2005; Artley, 1975) allow students to study words critically and conceptually. The Concept Circle is a categorizing activity. Students respond to the visual aspect of manipulating the sections of the circle.

Before Reading

Before reading, the teacher and students preview the text, noting the key vocabulary. The meanings of the words are predicted based on the title, subtitles, pictures, and captions. The vocabulary is then categorized.

During Reading

During reading, the students verify the meanings of the previously categorized words and take structured notes on their reading.

After Reading

After reading, the students are given Concept Circles. The teacher arranges one, two, or three forms on the student graphic organizer.

Working in learning groups or independently, students group words or phrases in the four sections of the circle, then name the concept they are illustrating. The students can work from a word bank if needed.

The teacher can modify this strategy by filling in all but one or two sections of the circle. The students then fill in the empty sections with words that relate in some way to the terms in the Concept Circle. The students name the concept on the blank below the circle.

Another variation has the teacher complete the circle terms and then the students review the terms, finding one term that does not relate to the concept. Students shade in or slash the term that does not belong. Again, students name the concept and are able to discuss the way terms are related.

Concept Circles

Directions: In the circles below, fill in the empty space with a term that relates to the other three terms. On the line, write what the four terms have in common.

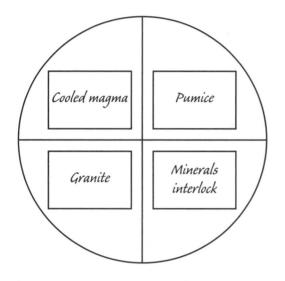

Cooled magma

Pumice

Granite

Minerals interlock

1. _____ Igneous rocks _____

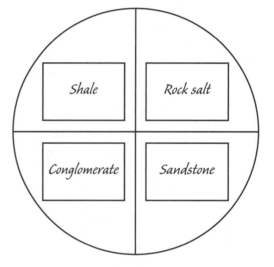

Shale

Rock salt

Conglomerate

Sandstone

2. _____ Sedimentary rocks _____

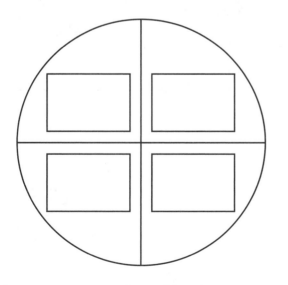

3. _____ Metamorphic rocks _____

Concept Circles

Directions: In the circles below, fill in the empty space with a term that relates to the other three terms. On the line, write what the four terms have in common.

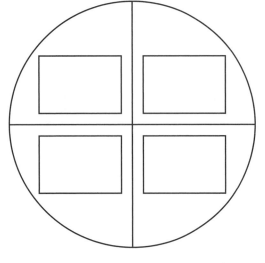

1. _____

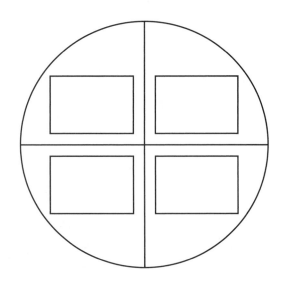

2. _____

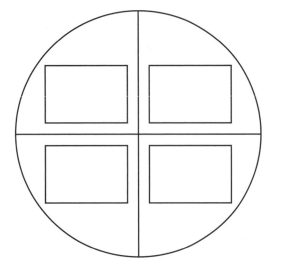

3. _____

EXPLANATION FOR APPLICATION OF READING STRATEGY

Frayer Model

The Frayer Model (Frayer, Frederick, & Klausmeier, 1969) helps students make connections between what they know and what they will be learning. Students learn to examine a concept from several perspectives: how the concept relates to other concepts and information and how to sort out the relevant features of a concept. Students classify more than one example of the concept, thereby extending their knowledge of the concept.

Before Reading

The teacher names the concept and students brainstorm examples, nonexamples, essential characteristics, and nonessential characteristics (as a class or in learning groups).

During Reading

As students read, they look for information to use in their Frayer Model, staying especially alert for facts and ideas that fit any of the four categories.

After Reading

Upon completion of the reading, students discuss their Frayer Models and concepts in a learning group. Class discussion clarifies the concept with respect to each of the four categories.

Frayer Model

Essential Characteristics

Things frogs have . . .

    Long tongue
    Webbed feet
    Four legs
    Moist skin

Nonessential Characteristics

Frogs can have . . .

    Gills
    Spots
    Tails

Frogs

Examples of Frogs

    Leopard frog
    Grass frog
    Tree frog

Examples That Are Not Frogs

    Toads
    Cats

Frayer Model

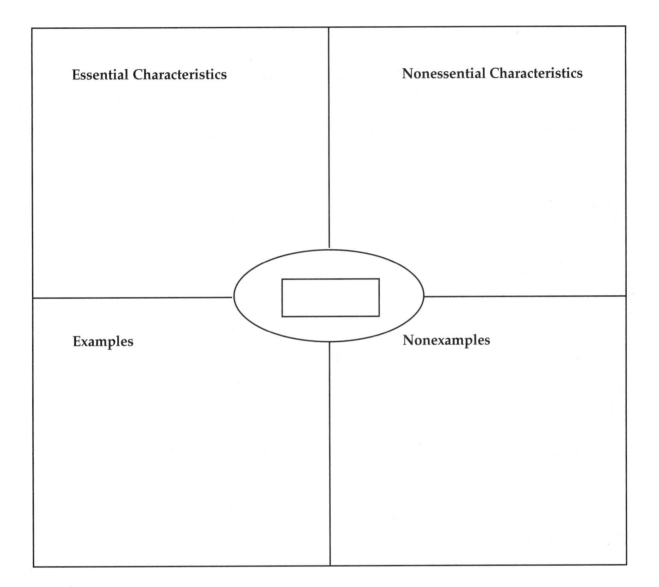

Content Area Cloze Procedure

A Cloze Procedure (Bluemfield & Miller, 1966) can help students learn to use context to infer word meanings. In a Cloze passage, selected words are omitted from the text (every fifth word is sometimes recommended) and replaced with a line or space. Reading a Cloze passage requires readers to use their knowledge of context to supply appropriate words in order to create a meaningful passage. This exercise can be used before or after reading the entire assignment. When used before reading, discussion can provide meaning for key terms; when completed after reading, the passage can be used to check understanding of concepts. Including a "Word Box" (an alphabetical listing of words to be used) for this activity is user friendly to ESL and struggling readers alike. To challenge remaining learners, omit the "Word Box" on other copies.

Before Reading

The teacher makes a transparency of a passage and omits contextually explained words. The teacher then directs the students to do the following:

- *Look* before, at, and after the word.
- *Reason* by connecting what they know with what the author has written.
- *Predict* a possible meaning. What word from students' personal vocabulary would sound right?
- *Read the first and last paragraph.* Decide what the author is trying to say.
- *Resolve or redo.* Decide if the students know enough about the topic or if they require support from a prereading strategy.

During Reading

Students read the assigned section.

After Reading

After reading, the students are given a Cloze Procedure passage with key concept words omitted. From the students' preview and reading of the text, they fill in the Cloze Procedure passage using the key concept terms. Remember, a word bank can be provided to support ESL, LD, or struggling readers.

Content Area Cloze Procedure

Word Box

a few centimenters	away from each other	continents	core
crust	earthquake	from each other	Himalaya
iron and nickel	mantle	Mid-Atlantic Ridge	mountains
new crust	plates	rock	
San Andreas Fault	toward each other	ways plates move	

The earth is made up of three layers. Earth's _____ is the layer we walk on. This layer is made up of the rock of the ocean floor and large areas of land called _____. Below the crust is the _____. It is the thickest layer. Most of this layer is made up of solid_____. Deep inside the Earth is the _____. The center is a dense ball made mostly of _____ and _____, two metals. The Earth's crust and upper mantle are broken into large slabs called _____. They move only _____ in distance a year. Plates can move in three ways, _____, _____, or _____. When plates move apart on the ocean floor, it forms _____. From plates moving apart in the Atlantic Ocean, a chain of mountains called _____ has formed. When plates move toward each other, _____ form. The _____ Mountains of Asia were formed in this way. Plates moving past each other can cause _____. This kind of plate movement happens along the _____ in California.

Source: Information from: *Harcourt Science. Grade 4*, p. C6–C8.

Magic Square

Magic Square (Vacca & Vacca, 2005) is a type of vocabulary matching activity that adds a novel twist: creating student interest.

Before Reading

Before reading, the teacher and students preview the chapter, section, or handout. Key vocabulary words are previewed and placed in categories. The meanings of the words are predicted based on the title, subtitles, pictures, and captions in the section.

During Reading

During reading, the students verify the meanings of the previously categorized words and take structured notes on their reading.

After Reading

After reading, the students are given a Magic Square graphic organizer. The terms and concepts are all related to the chapter or section they have just read. The activity has two columns, one for content area terms and one for definitions or other distinguishing statements, such as characteristics or examples.

The students match terms with definitions. Students must take into account the letters signaling the terms and the numbers signaling the definitions. The students put the number of a definition in the proper space, denoted by the letter of the term, into the Magic Square answer box.

The numerical total will be the same for each row across and each column down. It is this total that forms the puzzle's "Magic Number."

The students need to add up the rows and columns to check if they are coming up with the same number each time. If they do not get the same number for each row and column, they need to go back and reevaluate their answers.

Magic Square

Model of Magic Square Combinations

7	3	5
2	4	9
6	8	1

Magic Square Number = 15

8	1	6
3	5	7
4	9	2

Magic Square Number = 15

6	1	8
7	5	3
2	9	4

Magic Square Number = 15

16	2	3	13
5	11	10	8
9	7	6	12
4	14	15	1

Magic Square Number = 34

2	7	18	12
8	5	11	15
13	17	6	3
16	10	4	5

Magic Square Number = 39

19	2	15	23	6
25	8	16	4	12
1	14	22	10	18
7	20	3	11	24
13	21	9	17	5

Magic Square Number = 65

Source: From R. T. Vacca & J. L. Vacca, *Content Area Reading: Literacy and Learning across the Curriculum*, 8e. Published by Allyn and Bacon, Boston, MA. Copyright © 2005 by Pearson Education. Reprinted by permission of the publisher.

Magic Square

West Side Story

Directions: Select from the column on the right, the word or phrase that best matches the word or phrase on the left. Put the number of the match in the proper space in the Magic Square answer box. For instance, if the best match for (A) "Jets" is "an American gang," put "19" in the box marked (A). If your answers are correct, they will form a Magic Square. As incredible as it sounds, the total of the numbers will be the same in each row across and down to form a Magic Number.

A	B	C	D	E
F	G	H	I	J
K	L	M	N	O
P	Q	R	S	T
U	V	W	X	Y

A. Jets
B. Sharks
C. Riff
D. Maria
E. Bernardo
F. A-rab
G. Tony
H. Action
I. Anita
J. Doc
K. Velma
L. Anybodys
M. Glad Hand
N. bridal shop
O. dance at the gym
P. drug store
Q. killed Bernardo
R. Chino
S. stabbed Riff
T. in love with Tony
U. says, "ooblee-oo"
V. Diesel
W. tells Maria about her brother's death
X. ends the rumble
Y. the setting of the play

1. Riff's girl
2. a Puerto Rican gang
3. Bernardo wants Maria to marry him
4. Bernardo's girlfriend
5. the streets of New York
6. leader of the Sharks
7. where plans for the rumble are finalized
8. started the Jets with Riff
9. Chino
10. where Maria works
11. Bernardo
12. Tony works for him
13. Velma
14. a tomboy who wants to be a Jet
15. leader of the Jets
16. wanted to be Riff's "lieutenant"
17. police sirens
18. where Tony and Maria meet
19. an American gang
20. Tony
21. supposed to fight Bernardo in the rumble
22. tries to make the gangs dance
23. Bernardo's sister
24. Maria
25. Bernardo got revenge on him by piercing his ear.

Answer: Magic Square Number is 65. (See page 99.)

Magic Square

Directions: Select from the numbered statements the best answer for each of the terms. Put the number in the proper space of the Magic Square box. The total of the numbers will be the same across each row and down each column.

A	B	C
D	E	F
G	H	I

Terms	**Definition Match**
A.	1.
B.	2.
C.	3.
D.	4.
E.	5.
F.	6.
G.	7.
H.	8.
I.	9.

EXPLANATION FOR APPLICATION OF READING STRATEGY

Magnet Summaries

Magnet Summaries (Buehl, 2003) involve the identification of key terms or concepts—magnet words—from the reading of a selection or chapter. Students use the magnet words to organize important information that should be included in a summary.

Before Reading

Preview a short piece of text, looking at the title, headings, pictures, captions, introductions, summaries, and end questions. Then ask the students to identify a few key terms or concepts from the passage. Select the most important key term to demonstrate the process, showing the students that important vocabulary words are many times located in titles, subtitles, and highlighted words.

During Reading

After the students have read the short selection, ask the students to recall some important details that are related to the key magnet word and record them on the graphic organizer. These details can take the form of pictures, diagrams, or words. The students reread the text so that they can add important details that may have been missed. The teacher gives the students an additional two or three magnet words, and the students read the entire passage and generate important details for each magnet word.

After Reading

From classroom discussion, students continue to add information to their organizer. Next, the teacher demonstrates how to organize and combine the information into a sentence. The magnet word should be the main idea of the sentence. Unimportant details can be left out of the summary sentence.

Now the students work individually to make sentences for the other magnet words. After they have worked alone, they work with a partner on improving their summary sentences. The final step is to combine all of the Magnet Summary sentences into a summary paragraph. This is done by ordering the three to five summary sentences into a well-ordered paragraph.

Magnet Summaries

"Climbing Frozen Waterfalls"

Magnet Cards

Directions: Put key concept word in the middle of each card. As you read, put important details around the "magnet word."

walk slowly and heavily	exhausted
trudge	
deep snow	slippery ice

If you <u>trudge</u> through deep snow and walk slowly and heavily on slippery ice, you will be exhausted at the end of the day.

jagged	cut
serrated	
saw	teeth in an axe

When you use a <u>serrated</u> ax to climb frozen waterfalls, the ax has teeth that are jagged and cut and saw into the ice.

beginner	new
novice	
awkward	asks for help

A <u>novice</u> ice climber is a beginner who is new at the sport, so he or she must ask for advice and may be awkward the first few times he/she tries ice climbing.

spiritual	prayer-like
mystical experience	
Zen-like	addicting

The experience of ice climbing is <u>mystical</u> and spiritual because the climber goes into a prayer-like or Zen-like state of consciousness, which becomes addicting.

Arrange the four summary sentences into a paragraph summary.

To climb frozen waterfalls, the climber has to <u>trudge</u> through deep snow and walk slowly and heavily on slippery ice. This is very exhausting. One of the pieces of equipment that the climber must use is a <u>serrated</u> ax, which has teeth that are jagged and saw and cut into the ice. A <u>novice</u> ice climber is a beginner who is new at the sport, so he or she must ask for advice and may be awkward the first few times he/she tries climbing a frozen waterfall. Many ice climbers find the experience <u>mystical</u> or spiritual. They say that they go into a prayer-like or Zen-like state of consciousness, which becomes addicting.

Source: Information from Critical Reading Series, *Daredevils,* Jamestown Publishers, Chicago, IL.

Magnet Summaries

_____

Title of Selection

Magnet Cards

Put key concept word in the middle of each card. As you read, put important details around the "magnet word."

Write a summary of the key concept word and the surrounding details on the back of each card. Arrange the four summary sentences into a paragraph summary.

EXPLANATION FOR APPLICATION OF READING STRATEGY

Word Map

Word Maps (Schwartz & Raphael, 1985; Blachowicz & Fisher, 2002; Buehl, 2003) and charts are graphic representations that help students visualize the components of a definition. One type of Word Map is the Concept Definition Map. The map includes three relationships essential to a rich definition:

What is it?

What is it like?

What are some examples?

Word Maps teach students the qualities of a definition. Students are encouraged to personally integrate their background knowledge with a concept. Once students understand the qualities of a definition, they apply this knowledge to expand their own vocabularies and to master unfamiliar concepts.

Before Reading

In order to understand new vocabulary, students need to know what makes up a definition of a word. Introduce students to the Concept Definition Map. Begin with a familiar concept such as ice cream or preview our model on "Democracy."

During Reading

During reading, the students use the Concept Definition Map to define a key concept word. The word is placed in the center. Add words under the following three categories: "What is it?" "What is it like?" and "What are some examples?"

After Reading

The students share the likenesses and differences of their Word Maps in their learning groups. Students write one to three sentences defining the key concept word.

Word Map

Concept Definition Map

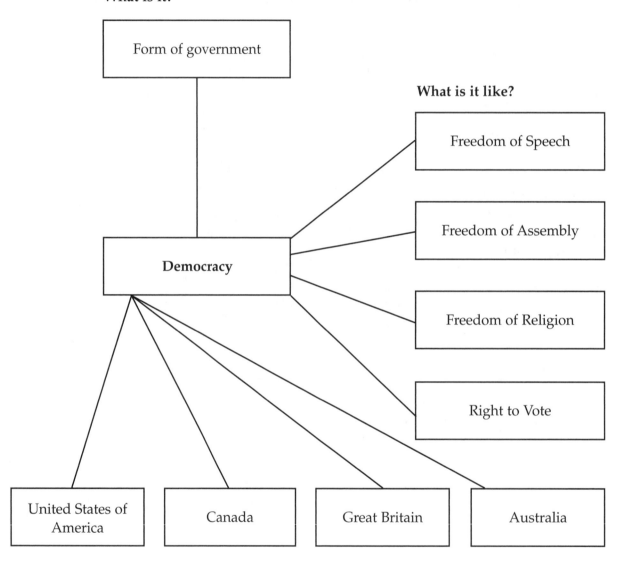

What is it?

Form of government

What is it like?

Freedom of Speech

Freedom of Assembly

Freedom of Religion

Right to Vote

Democracy

United States of America

Canada

Great Britain

Australia

What are some examples?

Word Map

Concept Definition Map

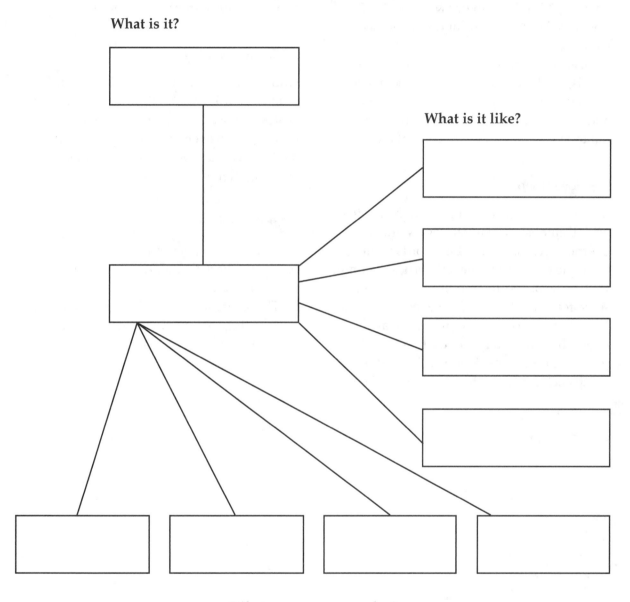

What is it?

What is it like?

What are some examples?

EXPLANATION FOR APPLICATION OF READING STRATEGY

Semantic Feature Analysis

Semantic Feature Analysis (Johnson & Pearson, 1984; Blachowicz & Fisher, 2002; Buehl, 2003) uses charts and grids to help students explore how words differ from one another. By analyzing semantic features of words, students can master important concepts that will help expand their vocabulary and help students understand words essential to learning concepts in content areas.

Before Reading

Identify the topic to be analyzed. Name the grid. Demonstrate this strategy using an overhead transparency. List words related to the topic category in the left vertical column. In the row across the top of the chart, list some features shared by some of the words. Model with students the process of analyzing each word in terms of each feature. Place plus or minus signs beside each word beneath each feature noting the appropriate relationship. Brainstorm with students any additional important words or features.

During Reading

Students read to confirm, clarify, and reformulate their ideas about the words and how Feature Analysis plays a part in word relationships. Answers can be changed during reading with a separate color of ink to show growing thought processes.

After Reading

Discuss any changes made to the Feature Analysis Chart. Compare prereading ideas with postreading thoughts.

This exercise can also be completed as a postreading tool. Student analysis of words is a valuable thinking skill.

Semantic Feature Analysis

"Six-Legged Wonders"

	Sings Rubs Body Parts	Eats Plants	Eats Animals and Insects	Has Wings and Flies	Has Wings Does Not Fly	Multi-color	Green Color	Black Color	Brown Color	Hard Shell Body	Soft Body
Cicadas	males	X		X				X		X	
Crickets	X	X			X			X		X	
Grasshoppers	X	X		X			X			X	
Katydids	X	X		X			X		X	X	
Cockroach		X	X		X				X	X	
Dragonfly			X	X		X					X
Ladybug			X	X		X	X			X	
Firefly		X		males				X			X

Source: Information from *The Contemporary Reader* (1998), Lincolnwood, IL: Jamestown Publishers, Vol. 2, N. 2, pp. 29–39.

Semantic Feature Analysis

Semantic Feature Analysis may be used as a cooperative reading strategy pairing challenged students as detectives to complete the missing facts. Teams contribute to the completion of a "Class Chart" either on oversized paper or an overhead transparency.

Advantages to this type of strategy include *excellent recall* of facts because each child is contributing to the research and recording as well as sharing information, leading to success for ESL, LD, and struggling readers.

Researching Biomes

Team members: _____

Biome	Location	Climate, Rainfall	Plant Example	Animal Example	Fact of Special Interest
tropical rain forest		hot, damp, very high			
deciduous forest				rabbit, skunks, deer, chipmunks	
grassland			grasses, grains		
		warm, very low	cactus, mesquite		
taiga					
		cool summer, cold winter, low		caribou, musk ox	

TEMPLATE FOR APPLICATION OF READING STRATEGY

Semantic Feature Analysis

Features → Words ↓						

CHAPTER FIVE

Talking to Learn

Talking to Learn Strategies

Guided Oral Discussion

Stop-the-Process
DRTA
Think-Pair-Share
Seed Discussion
Discussion Web
Jigsaw Activity

Fluency

Readers' Theater
Radio Reading

Talking to learn helps students explore, clarify, and think about ideas and concepts they encounter in reading and writing (Vacca & Vacca, 2005). The power of talk is often taken for granted, and therefore teachers do not realize the importance of using this medium for learning (Rubin, 1990). A policy statement prepared by the London Association for the Teaching of English stresses that talk not only shapes students' ideas but also causes them to modify their thinking through active listening (Barnes, Britten, & Rosin, 1969).

Research Preview
While reading researchers have defined reading comprehension in terms of text,

task, and subject contexts, the most important classroom influence on comprehension is the interaction between the students and the teacher (Mosenthal, 1984). In order for students to be actively engaged in discussion, they must talk at least 40 percent of the time, and this interaction should be among the students as well as with the teacher (Dillon, 1981). Vygotsky (1978) emphasized the social nature of learning and indicated that talk is a way to share knowledge and construct meaning between teachers and learners.

English Language Arts Standard

Students use spoken, written, and visual language to accomplish their own purposes (e.g., for learning, enjoyment, persuasion, and exchange of information) (NCTE/IRA, 1996). As a result of their schooling students will be able to listen and speak effectively in a variety of situations (Illinois State Board of Education, 1997).

Connections to Research

In the classroom, talk is the major form of communication among students and teacher. Often it becomes a recitation with the teacher asking a question and the student merely responding (Vacca & Vacca, 2005). In order for the process to effectively recognize the strength of speech in getting students to think creatively and critically, clarify ideas, and reflect on learning, there must be dialogue among participants rather than talk that is dominated by the teacher. Collaborative classroom discussion gives students the opportunity to question, plan, clarify, and explore meanings that connect literacy to learning. It is in these social exchanges that the power of talk positively impacts student learning.

In sociocultural theory (Mercer & Mercer, 1998; Bruner, 1990; Vygotsky, 1978), teaching and learning are culturally sensitive, interactive processes where teacher and learner play significant roles. The understandings that students develop are shaped by the interactions with peers and adults as well as the relationships that they create. While this theory stresses the importance of talk in learning, it does not take into consideration the process of moving from teacher-led to student-centered discussion. One study (Maloch, 2002) emphasized the importance of scaffolding student talk in ways that change the teacher's role to that of facilitator and the students' role to that of discussion leader. The teacher supports not only what is discussed but also how the discussion flows (Jewell & Pratt, 1999; Short, Kaufman, Kaser, Kahn, & Crawford, 1999). This study implies that the teacher plays a significant role in moving students from passive participants to active leaders in learning. The teacher uses literature discussion groups as the focus of the study. Table 5.1 (Maloch, 2002) shows the teacher's expectations and associated strategies.

One implication of this study stresses the need for teacher guidance in leading to new ways of interacting within the classroom. Teachers need to understand that students have difficulty shifting from recitation formats to that of leadership roles. Another implication of this research is that the teacher must assume a facilitative role within the classroom rather than the traditional leadership role. The teacher scaffolds the shared knowledge of conversation over time. This is necessary in order for students to move into the leadership role and successfully assume greater responsibility for collaborative learning.

Once teachers recognize the importance of using talk in the classroom as an overt means of developing understanding related to content area materials then they will consciously use this medium. Language is an important part of the social structure of the classroom. According to Halliday and Hasan (1976), three descriptors of situational

TABLE 5.1 • Teacher's Expectations and Associated Strategies

Teacher Goals and Expectations	Further Explanation of Goal	Strategies Associated with Goals

All members are involved and included in the discussion.	• Share own responses.
	• Invite others to share.
	• Acknowledge and value others' comments.
		• Ask questions, using names, to invite participation.
		• Acknowledge others' comments by:
		  (a) asking follow-up question.
		  (b) restating to check your understanding.
		  (c) thanking person for sharing.
		• Enter conversation by using follow-up question, generating a response topic or question, or connecting with a previous comment (by saying "I agree" or "I disagree").

The discussion is cohesive.	• Responses or turns are linguistically and/or semantically connected. • Cohesive discussions are often characterized by longer amounts of time on a particular topic.	• Ask follow-up questions that continue or expand a line of thought (e.g., "Why do you think that?" or "What else . . . ?"). • Use responsive phrases such as "I agree/disagree because" or "like Nancy said" to connect to another's comment and help members follow line of discussion. • Make semantic/meaning connections between speakers and between topics.
Discussion participants generate substantive discussion topics.	• Students will generate topics for discussion. • Discussion topics will be substantive (help generate in-depth conversations).	• Refer to literature response log for topics to share. • Refer to book (i.e., illustrations, interesting quotes) for topics to share. • Generate your own topics that relate to existing discussion.
The discussion focuses on one common topic or text at a time.	• Discussion centers around a shared piece of text. • Discussion is closely related to book, although personal connections are stressed. • Discussion centers on one common topic at a time.	• Identify page numbers or section of book (if there is one) that sparked a question. • Retell story. Monitor discussion and alert members when off-task (e.g., "You're getting off-track" or "The book doesn't have anything to do with . . . ").
Participants support responses by sharing reasoning.	• Share reasoning or book evidence to support response. • Invite others to share reasoning.	• Ask follow-up questions (e.g., "Why do you say that?") when participants use one-word or nondescript answers. • Include reasoning in your responses. • Share book quotes, when appropriate, to support responses.

Source: Maloch, Beth. (Jan/Feb/March 2002). Scaffolding student talk: One teacher's role in literature discussion groups. *Reading Research Quarterly, 37*(1), 94–112. Reprinted with permission of Beth Maloch and the International Reading Association.

context characterize the social environment of text. First, is the "field of discourse," which is the nature of the social action in which language plays a crucial role. Second, in the "tenor of discourse," which relates to the roles and relationships of the participants. Third, is the "mode of discourse," which describes the part that language is playing and the channel (oral and written) that is used. The "field" (experiential), "tenor" (interpersonal), and "mode" (textual) provide the framework for interpreting the social exchanges of meaning through language (Halliday, 1978). Conversation in the classroom is more unique when talk becomes a planned strategy to enhance literacy and thereby increase learning. According to Falk-Ross (1997), students with language difficulties can also benefit through these participation strategies as teachers and students use talk in questioning, commenting, and clarifying information.

Various strategies that emphasize talking to learn are described in the next paragraphs. They can be used with all major content areas such as language arts, mathematics, science, social science, fine arts, foreign language, physical education, and health. These strategies reflect the facilitative role of the teacher in encouraging student leadership roles for collaborative discussion of content, including the materials associated with the content.

Stop-the-Process (Katz, 1999; Frank, 2001), an adaptation of a Directed Reading Thinking Activity, is a strategy that proves useful with difficult text. The students are given a graphic organizer composed of six squares, each of which contains a teacher's prompt. Each prompt also indicates the text pages that students are expected to read. Students may be asked to answer a question, respond to a drawing, define a word, or make a prediction. The page numbers that they are to read signal the appropriate time to stop and respond to the prompt. This is also an effective strategy to use in preparing for a test covering the material in their content area reading class. The important part of this entire process is to provide time for students to respond to the prompt, but then to allow additional time for them to share their responses with their partners. It is during this talking phase that greater clarification of content occurs. This helps to ensure all class members understand difficult concepts.

The Directed Reading Thinking Activity (DRTA) (Stauffer, 1969; Davidson & Wilkerson, 1988) engages students in dialogue about the selection they are reading. Students are asked to address three questions in the process of reading. First, they talk about what they think the reading selection is about. Secondly, they explain why they feel this is the case. Thirdly, they are asked if they can prove it. The teacher determines at which points along the way to stop the students and discuss their reading in response to these three questions. It is beneficial to break difficult text into segments to help clarify the students' understanding of sections as they read and discuss the material. At the end of the reading selection, the teacher asks the students if they were right about their predictions concerning what would happen. Students are pleased when they understood the author's purpose in the reading selection.

Think-Pair-Share (Kagan, 1989) is a discussion strategy because it involves everyone as a participant in the process. This can be used in a prereading activity, during a lecture, for problem solving, or as follow-up to the lesson. The teacher presents a question or topic of study. The students think about the topic or question and then write down what they know. They then partner with another classmate and share their ideas or understanding related to the topic. After they share their knowledge about the topic with the partner, they may further expand their understanding through the collaboratively broadened perspective of discussion with the entire class. This is extremely valuable prior to reading a very difficult selection of text.

Seed Discussions (Vallaume et al., 1994; Santa et al., 2004) provide ways for students to lead discussions about what they are reading. The students write down an important aspect of what they are reading. As each student presents his or her seed (idea) for discussion, others in the class have a chance to share their thoughts regarding that idea. All comments are shared before moving to the next idea. This elaboration on class members' ideas helps to verify understanding associated with the text they are reading. The more students can discuss their reading, the more likely they are to gain greater clarification of the content.

A **Discussion Web** (Alvermann, 1991; Buehl, 2003) is a strategy to help students participate in an organized discussion that contains opposing points of view. This "talking to learn" activity involves 100% of the students in thinking, reading, gathering information, drawing conclusions, and discussing. The graphic framework for the Discussion Web helps students organize data to recognize various points of view. The teacher proposes a statement that students can explore from both the pro and con side, such as *"Chopping down the rainforest destroys the environment and hurts the indigenous people"* or *"The U.S. Civil War was really fought over the issue of states' rights."*

The students read the statement and the assigned text. They record evidence for supporting "yes" or "no" to the statement. They meet with a partner to discuss the recorded facts and then with groups of four to evaluate the data and synthesize their ideas. The groups decide which side of the issue has the most evidence and then write a conclusion. From this collaboration, a class discussion ensues.

A **Jigsaw** (Aronson, 1978; Slavin, 1988) divides the responsibilities among a team.

Members of each small group are responsible for reading a section of text and teaching that material to their group. This differentiation of instruction creates an expert on the topic assigned. The expert then assumes responsibility for sharing knowledge with others members of his or her team. The team then develops a summary that provides a complete description of their section of the article to the entire class. This reduces the amount of reading required and determines who will lead the discussion on the topic. By more participants assuming responsibility for various segments of a text, greater clarification of the content occurs. This shared ownership in the discussion of the text gets everyone engaged in the dialogue. Greater understanding of content occurs as a result of using this strategy.

Readers' Theater (Rasinski, 2001) gives students the opportunity to write their own script from books and stories they have read. They then have a chance to act out their scripts. This provides an opportunity for students to work on fluency and expressive reading. As they practice their scripts, the students project the characters' emotional state and personality to the audience. It is a way for small groups who are reading a similar story or book to integrate writing and drama and then verbalize the dialogue to the entire class. It is important to work with the students to create a collaborative script initially so that the process is modeled.

Radio Reading (Artley, 1975) is a strategy to get students to listen actively to what another individual reads and then respond. Students should make sure that they have their own books closed when a classmate is reading. The reader directs the conversation by asking questions of the group in order to generate discussion. The teacher may need to facilitate the students' dialogue in moving from literal questions to those of a higher-level thinking category. A secretary can be appointed to record who responded to the questions as well as to provide a summary of each response. Students take turns being the reader as they cover various components of the text. This is most effective to use with a guided reading group in language arts. This gives everyone the opportunity to be a reader, listener, discussion leader, conversationalist, and recorder. It certainly helps to cement understandings of concepts or content presented.

Talking to learn provides powerful strategies to clarify student understanding of narrative as well as content area reading. By breaking text down into smaller components with students engaged in discussion or dialogue surrounding the text, more meaning is derived. As a result, students experience greater comprehension of the material that they are expected to learn. Shared leadership for learning becomes an expected form of discourse within the classroom.

EXPLANATION FOR APPLICATION OF READING STRATEGY

Stop-the-Process

Stop-the-Process (Katz, 1999; Frank, 2001) strategy is an adaptation of DRTA. Students are given the graphic organizer with six squares, each containing a teacher-directed prompt. The prompts tell the students specific pages to read and then give them specific prompts for those pages. The prompts call for an answer to a question, a drawing, a listing of interesting words, or a prediction. The teacher previews the material to determine stopping points for the reader—the place where the reader will have enough information to answer the prompt. The students are timed as they read and respond to each prompt. They are then given two minutes to share their responses to the prompt with a partner. Teachers could make use of end questions from the chapter as prompts or use test questions from the unit as a focus for the prompts. Modeling with your class using the organizer and the overhead is the best introduction for this strategy.

Before Reading

Begin by previewing chapter titles, subheadings, illustrations, and charts with the students. Introduce the first prompt in the first box. Students are timed as they read the assigned pages and respond to the prompt.

During Reading

The students reread the prompt from the first box, noting the text pages to be covered. If the teacher chooses, "Post-it" notes could be available for students to mark where an answer or supportive information is found; this is especially helpful to more challenged learners. The response is recorded in the appropriate box. Then students are given two minutes to share their response with their partner. The process continues for each subsequent prompt.

After Reading

This six-square Stop-the-Process is then used as a basis for classroom discussion or summary writing.

Stop-the-Process

How the Earth and Moon Interact

Chapter _____

Name:

Read pages ___-___.

1. Describe a new moon.

Read pages ___-___.

2. Draw a lunar eclipse.

Read pages ___-___.

3. Draw a solar eclipse.

4. Read pages ___-___. Compare a solar eclipse to a lunar eclipse.

_____

_____

_____

_____

_____

---

5. What do you see from Earth during a total lunar eclipse? Describe or draw, include the correct phase of the moon.

_____

_____

_____

_____

(Use back if you need more room.)

6. Which of these is NOT a phase of the moon?

   a. new

   b. crescent

   c. full

   d. eclipse

TEMPLATE FOR APPLICATION OF READING STRATEGY

Stop-the-Process

Name _____ **Date** _____

Title _____

1. Read pages ___-___.	2. Read pages ___-___.
3. Read pages ___-___.	4. Read pages ___-___.
5. Read pages ___-___.	6. Read pages ___-___.

EXPLANATION FOR APPLICATION OF READING STRATEGY

Directed Reading Thinking Activity (DRTA)

DRTA (Stauffer, 1969; Richek et al., 2002) focuses the student on the content and purpose for reading a particular text. The teacher sets the climate for the DRTA and directs the process with the frequent use of these three questions:

What do you think the story (selection) is about?

Why do you think so?

Can you prove it?

This strategy works well with content area as well as narrative text. The teacher predetermines "reading stops" at points where the reader has enough information to predict a future happening.

Before Reading

Before reading, the teacher directs the students to read the story title, look at the pictures, and check the end questions. Then, using personal experiences and background knowledge, the student sets the purpose for reading by answering the questions: "What do you think the story (selection) is about?" and "Why do you think so?" Making the best prediction possible, the purpose and focus for initial reading is set. At the choice of the teacher, this prediction may or may not be written out on a strategy page.

During Reading

Once the class has set the purpose, reads to test the prediction, and reevaluates the purpose in light of the first page or two of reading, the teacher repeats the questions: "What do you think this story (selection) is about?" and "Why do you think so?" The instructor asks, "How do you know?" to help clarify and verify ideas. The predictions are recorded on the board or on a transparency.

The students continue silent reading to the next stopping point. The teacher asks similar questions and records the students' predictions. As the students stop reading, the predictions are evaluated by using reflective questions, such as: " Were you right?" "Can you prove it?" "What made you think that?" or "Where did you get on the wrong track?" After guiding the students through the predictions, the teacher asks for a new hypothesis about the story development on the basis of what is now known.

After Reading

At the conclusion of the reading, the teacher asks "Were you right in what you thought would happen?" The students' final analysis of what will happen is usually very close to the author's purpose.

MODEL FOR APPLICATION OF READING STRATEGY

Directed Reading Thinking Activity (DRTA)

Title _____ **The Thing at Exeter** _____

Initial prediction: What do you think this story (selection) will be about?

I think this story is about an unidentified flying object.

Why do you think so?

In the first paragraph, it said that the Air Force reported that at that time no aircraft were in the area of Exeter, New Hampshire.

Read to the bottom of page ___. What do you think this story (selection) will be about?

It will be about how Norman Muscarello goes to the police and tells them about the strange object he saw in the night sky.

Why do you think so?

Norman is frightened by the object and asks an older couple to drive him to the police station.

Read to the bottom of page ___. What do you think this story (selection) will be about?

The police go to investigate the flying object with the bright red light, and the police also see the object.

Why do you think so?

A police officer named Bertrand drove Norman back to the place where he saw the flying object.

Can you prove it?

They were going back to the site together and a second officer was joining them. The animals in a nearby barn started howling and making noises.

Read to the end of the selection. Were you right in what you thought would happen?

Yes, the two officers and Norman saw the flying object that moved in the sky without making any sound. Its lights were extremely bright. The Air Force said that they did not have any craft in the area at 1:35 a.m. I am right in thinking that this is a story about UFOs.

TEMPLATE FOR APPLICATION OF READING STRATEGY

Directed Reading Thinking Activity (DRTA)

Title _____

Initial prediction: What do you think this story (selection) will be about?

Why do you think so?

Read to the bottom of page ___. What do you think this story (selection) will be about?

Why do you think so?

Read to the bottom of page ___. What do you think this story (selection) will be about?

Why do you think so?

Can you prove it?

Read to the end of the selection. Were you right in what you thought would happen?

EXPLANATION FOR APPLICATION OF READING STRATEGY

Think-Pair-Share

This discussion strategy, Think-Pair-Share (Kagan, 1989), is especially supportive of learning since every student is an engaged participant. It works well with content area and narrative, or as a problem-solving strategy. It is important for teachers to decide the primary purpose for using the strategy. The information from discussion can be used to predict events or facts in an upcoming reading or to form an after-reading summary. The components are quite simple; learners engage in scaffolding meaning of text.

This model allows time for thought; students consider their response and make connections to the world they understand. By allowing time for thought and reaction, a fuller, richer, and more thoughtful discussion will result.

Before Reading

Students preview the lesson material before reading. Then, the teacher begins by posing the study topic or a question. Students think and then write down what they know or have learned about the topic. After writing down their thoughts, students "pair" with another assigned student, share their thinking, and come to consensus.

During Reading

Students read silently to clarify, verify, or modify their thinking.

After Reading

The teacher puts student answers on the board. A whole-class "share" discussion follows. This discussion can be a springboard to construct a summary of material if the teacher so desires.

Think-Pair-Share

Name _____ **Date** _____

"Pair" partner is: _seatmate_ _____

Please review before beginning:

- Be a courteous listener.
- Look at the speaker.
- Allow your partner to complete sharing without interruption.
- Compare thinking with facts from text.

Topic or question:

Animals have adaptations that help them meet their needs in many ways. Consider body parts, body coverings, shape, size, color, and basic needs of animals in their environment. Be ready to discuss this information.

My thoughts:

What I know or have learned on this particular topic . . .

Hawks have talons to grasp their prey while in flight, the chameleon's skin allows it to blend with its environment in minutes for protection, a praying mantis resembles a twig saving it from enemies, and a porcupine's quills keep its enemies at bay. Also the beaks of birds determine their diet and many animals grow heavier fur to withstand the cold climate during winter.

Notes on "Pair" discussion:

Our discussion compared the behavior of many animals like those listed above, but we also brought up the part that instinct plays in the survival of animals. We had quite a discussion on instinct versus behavior learned from the caretaker.

TEMPLATE FOR APPLICATION OF READING STRATEGY

Think-Pair-Share

Name _____ **Date** _____

"Pair" partner is: _____

Please review before beginning:

- Be a courteous listener.
- Look at the speaker.
- Allow your partner to complete sharing without interruption.
- Compare thinking with facts from text.

Topic or question:

_____
_____

My thoughts:
What I know or have learned on this particular topic . . .

_____
_____
_____
_____
_____

Notes on "Pair" discussion:

_____
_____
_____

EXPLANATION FOR APPLICATION OF READING STRATEGY

Seed Discussion

Vallaume et al. (1994) (Santa et al., 2004) shared one way to help students learn to lead their own discussions through "Seed" Discussions. Students also learn appropriate behavior to participate in discussions as courteous encouragers. This strategy works well with content area subjects as well as narrative or poetry genre.

As students read the material assigned, each is asked to "write down one thing they understand." Begin the discussion by having the first author of a "seed" present one idea. Then, everyone in the group comments about the idea before the next person presents a "seed" of understanding. Introduce this strategy by modeling several of your own discussion "seeds." As students understand the procedure and begin their own discussion groups, ask that they work in groups of four. Assign roles to involve all learners. Each group member is an encourager, using phrases such as: "I like what you said about . . . ," "I agree with you . . . ," or Maybe we should consider. . . . The following individual roles are suggested:

> Manager: Make sure each member has the Seed Discussion organizer to write their "seed" for discussion.
>
> Leader: Call on each member to share a "seed" of discussion.
>
> Checker: See that each group member has a chance to comment on each "seed."
>
> Reporter: Report to the teacher when the discussion is complete.

Before Reading

Students are given the Seed Discussion organizer and the passage, chapter, or assignment they are responsible to read.

During Reading

As students read, they identify and think about topics they feel are important in some way. Each student writes one thing he or she understands from reading the assignment. (Variations might include one thing the student had a difficult time understanding, one thing that was interesting, or one thing that was surprising.)

After Reading

At the conclusion of reading and writing, students are divided into groups of four. Roles are assigned and the discussion begins by having the first author of the "seed" present one idea. Then, everyone in the group comments about the idea before the next person presents a "seed" of understanding. The reporter lets the teacher know when the discussion is complete. The teacher may elect to end at this point or have a full class discussion, sharing the major "seed" that each group agrees to contribute.

Seed Discussion

Name _____ **Date** _____

Group # _____

Assignment _Social Studies, page_ _____ : _The Gold Rush_ _____

My group role is that of _Encourager,_ **plus (circle one):**

Manager: Make sure each group member has the organizer to write their "seed" for discussion.

Leader: Call on each member to share a "seed" of discussion.

Checker: See that each group member has a chance to comment on each "seed."

Reporter: Report to the teacher when the discussion is complete.

One thing I understand is:

The gold seekers came from all over the world to California in 1849 and were referred to as the

"forty niners."

_____

_____

_____

_____

TEMPLATE FOR APPLICATION OF READING STRATEGY

Seed Discussion

Name _____ **Date** _____

Group # _____

Assignment _____

My group role is that of *Encourager,* **plus (circle one):**

Manager: Make sure each group member has the organizer to write their "seed" for discussion.

Leader: Call on each member to share a "seed" of discussion.

Checker: See that each group member has a chance to comment on each "seed."

Reporter: Report to the teacher when the discussion is complete.

One thing I understand is:

_____

_____

_____

_____

_____

_____

Discussion Web

Discussion Web (Alvermann, 1991; Buehl, 2003; Santa, 2004) is a strategy to help students discuss textual material containing opposing points of view. Informational, narrative, and most content area text can be adapted to this format, which will move the focus from teacher-dominated discussion to student-centered interpretation and reasoning in active verbal exchanges.

The graphic framework for the Discussion Web helps students organize their thoughts about ideas from text. The central question is stated in such a way that students can explore the pros and cons of an issue. Students learn to collaborate on pros and cons in pairs, then move on to groups of four to discuss their views and reach a conclusion based on evidence.

The teacher reviews the text material to create the "Focus Question," making sure the focus is broad enough, yet challenging and lends itself to discussion, both factual and experiential in nature.

Before Reading

Introduce the Discussion Web and ask students to work in pairs to analyze a target question.

During Reading

Students read the selection and gather evidence that supports the pro or con point of view from text. Partners can then work on combining their pro and con evidence, writing it down on the organizer.

After Reading

Now partners become groups of four to compare all responses and to collaborate on determining which side of the issue has the most evidence. Select a spokesperson for each group. The teacher now leads the class discussion. Teachers may follow up the class discussion with individual writing.

Discussion Web

A Wave of Immigration

Positive

Farmers came for better farmland—they couldn't grow enough food to feed their family.

Some came to practice their own religion.

Dancing, singing on ships

Children went to school and picked up English easily.

Usually lived in immigrant neighborhoods

Speak native language

Job connections

Stores sold items from their home country

Signs written in native language

Learn about other cultures

Learn tolerance and respect for other cultures

Opportunity to make a new life

Focus Question
The life of an immigrant to the United States in the late 1800s and early 1900s had both good and difficult times. From your reading, record some of those contributing factors.

Conclusion
Even though they suffered many hardships, immigrants continued to seek a new life in a new country.

Negative

The ships were terribly overcrowded, smelly, unhealthy

Immigrants became sick as they traveled

Family members left behind

Had to learn a new language

Had to learn new jobs

Change from farm laborer to city work

Living in crowded apartments

Hearing city noises rather than the morning crow of the rooster

Homesickness

Learning to live alongside other cultures

Many only brought the clothes on their back

Left behind many valued objects and family

The United States welcomes many immigrants today. They experience similar things in getting used to life in the United States. Name a few things today's immigrants have in common with the immigrants of the 1890s and 1920s.

Today's immigrants still need to learn to speak the language and need to be trained for new types of jobs. They also leave behind valued objects and loved family members.

Discussion Web

Pros _____

_____

_____

_____

_____

Focus Question _____

_____

_____

_____

Cons _____

_____

_____

_____

Conclusion _____

_____

_____

Best support of conclusion:

_____

_____

EXPLANATION FOR APPLICATION OF READING STRATEGY

Jigsaw

The purpose of the Jigsaw strategy is to create close working relationships among teammates (Aronson, 1978; Slavin, 1988). Jigsaw groups are composed of students divided heterogeneously into three to five member teams. Each team member will become an expert on one section of text or one subtopic of a theme under study. Each student is accountable for teaching his or her topic to the team and for learning the information other team members provide and discuss. In the exercise that follows, students are learning about the "Black Plague." Each team is assigned a short segment of the overall passage. Each segment is divided into sections and assigned a topic (main idea) by the teacher. Each student on the team is given a segment to read, summarize, and teach to the rest of the team. Then the team will compose a summary of the segments to share with the class. Each team will present and teach their data as sequenced by the original text. All teammates and all classmates will understand the material with input from each person.

Before Reading

Form small learning teams, assign the text selection, and assign team members a segment of text to be read (i.e., segment A, B, C, or D). Several minutes are given for reading by each group member as well as time for note taking and summarizing.

During Reading

Each team member reads, takes notes, and creates a summary of his or her assigned segment of text.

After Reading

All of the students reading segment A form a group, all reading segment B form a group, all reading segment C form a group, and all reading segment D form a group. Each of these teams collaborates to form a summary of their segment. Now students return to their original teams composed of an A, B, C, and D member to develop the final summary. This final and all-inclusive summary is recorded on a transparency and shared with the entire class.

Jigsaw

Name _____ Date _____

Title: _____ **Black Plague** _____

"Team A" segment of the passage to read and master is (copy, clip, and glue section here):

Burial of Victims

So many people were struck down by the plague that the supply of coffins was soon exhausted, and the dead were carried on wooden planks to huge mass-burial pits. Corpses were piled several high, and then a thin layer of dirt was shoveled over them. Often burials took place with no member of the family or clergy present. As people fled before the spreading plague, spouse abandoned spouse, and parents forsook children.

Speed of the Disease

The plague spread quickly from person to person. People went to bed well and were dead by morning. A doctor might arrive at a home to treat a victim only to catch the plague and die before the original sufferer.

Symptoms of the Disease

The Black Death derived its name from the color of the victim's skin in death; a person who was infected always died within three days, skin covered by black patches. There were other symptoms, too. Patients developed egg-size swellings in the groin and armpits. Sometimes victims also coughed and sweated violently.

Brief summary of "Team A" passage information (main idea):

Burial of Victims	Speed of the Disease	Symptoms of the Disease
The many corpses were piled high in huge mass-burial pits.	The plague spread so quickly that people went to bed well and were dead by morning.	Swelling in the lymph areas, violent coughing, sweating, and black patches on the skin of the dead were symptoms.

Group summary contributions: Using the information under each heading, write a paragraph summarizing the information. Create a sentence for each heading.

The Black Plague spread so quickly that people went to bed well and were dead by morning. Symptoms include swelling in the lymph areas, violent coughing and sweating and the typical black patches on the skin of the infected. So many people were struck by the disease that corpses were piled high in mass burial pits and covered with a thin layer of dirt.

Other segments of Black Plague are simultaneously being summarized by teams B, C, and D. Next students return to their original teams, composed of an A, B, C, and D member, to develop the final summary. This all-inclusive summary is recorded on a transparency and shared with the entire class.

Note: Information from Jamestown Publishers (1999), *Disasters: Critical Reading Series.*

Jigsaw

Title _____   **Date** _____   **Name** _____

Team ____ **segment of the passage to read and summarize is:**

Brief summary of Team ____ **passage information** (main idea):

_____   _____   _____

Group summary contributions: Using the information under each heading, write a paragraph summarizing the information. Create a sentence for each heading.

Other segments of the text are simultaneously being summarized by teams B, C, and D. Next students return to their original teams, composed of an A, B, C, and D member, to develop the final summary. This final and all-inclusive summary is recorded on a transparency and shared with the entire class.

EXPLANATION FOR APPLICATION OF READING STRATEGY

Readers' Theater

Readers' Theater (RT) provides readers with a legitimate reason to reread text and to practice fluency. RT promotes cooperative interaction with peers and makes the reading task appealing, as in Put Reading First, a booklet published by the U.S. Department of Education and others (2001). Timothy Rasinski (2001) of Kent State University has been at the forefront of Readers' Theater for years. Readers' Theater is defined as an orally read performance of a script in which meaning is conveyed through the readers' expressive and interpretive reading (and not through movement, memorization, props, or costumes). This strategy can be implemented for fun or as support for a content area topic or literacy unit theme. Websites are available for scripts and are listed at the end of this strategy. More advanced students could develop their own script from authentic literature.

The teacher chooses an appropriate text for the oral performance. For optimal fluency, students are given time for rehearsal. The focus for the script becomes the interpretation, conveying meaning through expression and intonation, rather than through memorization of text.

Give each student a copy of the script to read over as any piece of literature. Then assign individuals or groups to read various parts of the script for rehearsal. Reread with greater expression. Next is a class performance with students chosen to read the various parts. They can be positioned at the front of the class in order of the character's

importance. At the conclusion, students state their names and the parts that they read.

Before Reading

The teacher selects an appropriate script for the interest and abilities of the class as a whole. The greatest benefit comes when the activity is tied to a unit of study or theme the class is focusing on. Students are given a copy of the script to read and reread, practicing their delivery of script.

During Reading

Readers attend to the stage direction (if any) and attempt to reproduce the character's expression. Remember the focus for the script becomes the interpretation, conveying meaning through expression and intonation, rather than memorization of text. Choral reading can be used as rehearsal to develop expression and fluency.

After Reading

After many rehearsals to gain fluency and expression, the teacher may elect to have a class performance. Students are chosen to read various parts. They can be positioned at the front of the class in order of the character's importance. At the conclusion, students state their names and the parts that they read. Consider videotaping the performance for student enjoyment, to note fluency, and to reflect on the rehearsal necessary to gain that fluency.

Readers' Theater

Experiencing World-Wide Habitats: Selected from Four Continents

Directions: Using the following "Experiencing World-Wide Habitats" text, assign each student a voice to rehearse and read aloud as a Readers' Theater. This can be used in conjunction with any field trip involving unusual animals.

Southeast Asia

Narrator: We will be taking you on a journey to visit four continents. We will pay special attention to several animals from a variety of habitats that we think you will find unusual. Southeast Asia has some extremely interesting animals with which we would like you to become familiar. Try to picture these animals as you listen.

Voice 1: Nine feet long with powerful jaws,

Voice 2: My tail is wide for swimming.

Voice 3: As an aquatic lizard, I eat . . .

Voice 4: Small rodents, other lizards, and fish.

Voices 1 and 3: I am the **Malayan water monitor** of Indonesia.

Voice 5: I am an **Asian small-clawed otter.**

Voice 6: Reaching out with my paws, I catch my prey, feasting on fish and crabs.

Voice 7: I am so intelligent; I can be trained to catch and bring fish to my owner!

Voice 8: I am a *massive* snake, and I grow to 13 feet.

Voice 9: The longest ever is 19 feet—give me room!

Voice 10: As an **Indian python,** I eat deer, monkeys, and goats.

Voices 8, 9, and 10: I am becoming extinct, habitat destruction may force an end to me.

Africa

Narrator: Now we are off to Africa to hear about three unusual animals found on *this* far away continent. Are you trying to visualize how each animal may appear?

Voice 11: **Rock hyrax,** that's my name.

Voice 12: I'm the size of a rabbit, but related to, the elephant!

Voice 13: I live in the Sahara and have suction-like foot pads,

Voice 14: To help me run up steep boulders, with agility and quickness.

Voice 15: Hatched out of an egg 11 inches long, I grow to 6 feet.

Voice 16: Rain forests, swamps, and rivers of West Africa are where you'll find me.

Voice 17: I lie motionless, almost submerged, to attack unsuspecting fish and amphibians. I have to eat, you know!

Voices 15, 16, and 17: An armored reptile am I, the **African dwarf crocodile.** Endangered!

Voice 18: **Naked mole rat** living in the desert,

Voice 19: Dwelling in an underground labyrinth,

Voice 20: My place includes special sleeping rooms and nurseries for the little ones.

Voice 21: A single female dominates, much as a queen bee.

Voice 22: Other animals are soldiers or workers, who protect the queen and her nest, clean underground tunnels, and gather food.

South America

Narrator: South America is our next stop. These unique animals sound very exciting to get to know, from a distance! Try

Readers' Theater (continued)

to imagine what each might look like as you listen.

Voice 1: I'm a **dyeing poison arrow frog.**

Voice 2: Watch out! Extremely potent poison is excreted through my skin.

Voice 3: My brilliant colors make me a jewel of the rainforest,

Voice 4: Warning predators away.

Voice 5: Deforestation in Brazil endangers me.

Voice 6: I am the **golden-headed lion tamarin.**

Voice 7: I've a long and silky mane.

Voice 8: We mate for life; we usually produce twins.

Voice 9: As a **three-banded armadillo,** my back is protected by strong bony body plates,

Voice 10: But my underbelly is covered with soft, hairy skin.

Voice 11: To protect myself from predators I roll into . . .

Voice 12: A complete, armored ball.

Australia

Narrator: Our final visit is to the continent of Australia. We have located some interesting animals here as well. Listen carefully!

Voice 13: Having no teeth, my long sticky tongue

Voice 14: Removes ants and termites from their nests. Yum, yum.

Voice 15: Using excellent hearing, and my sharp keen smell,

Voice 16: I detect my enemies, safely curling into a tight, spiny ball.

Voice 17: **The short-nosed echina,** I am one of the world's two egg-laying mammals.

Voices 13, 14, 15, 16, and 17: Do you know the other?

(It's a duck-billed platypus.)

Voice 18: A marsupial, not a bear, I am a **koala.**

Voice 19: Weighing in at birth at half a gram, I'm the size of a bee.

Voice 20: After living in Mom's pouch for six months,

Voice 21: I spend the rest of my life high in a eucalyptus tree.

Voice 22: A diet of eucalyptus is my only food and drink.

Voices, All:

Growing to six feet in length,
the **green tree python,**
spends its entire life,
coiling around branches, in treetops.
A constrictor,
it loves the high temperature,
and tropical humidity,
of northern Australia.

Narrator: We've enjoyed bringing you new information on various worldwide habitats. Imagining what animals might look like can be fun! Look for these animals on the internet—view pictures and further information. One site to try is the Lincoln Park Zoo in Chicago: www.lpzoo.com.

Website resources for readers' theater: http://www.aaronshep.com/rt/; http://www. readers-theatre.com; http://www.storycart.com; http://loiswalker.com/catalog/guidesamples.html; http://www.readinglady.com; http://home.spynet.com/~palermo/into_rdio.htm.

Note: Information from *Creatures of Habitat,* Lincoln Park Zoo, Chicago, IL. Readers' theater script composed by Cecilia Frank and Jan Grossi.

Readers' Theater

Directions: Model your Readers' Theater after a story you have enjoyed or make up your own plot. Try choral reading or echo some of the dialogue as a format. Use poetry or prose style. This organizer can assist as you plot your ideas for characters and narrators. Use character names or the speaker numbers provided. Many times the narrator sets up the beginning of the play and the characters speak to the plot. Move the speaking slots around to suit your purposes. Enjoy your Readers' Theater creation, repeating your readings to add expression and fluency.

Character parts to assign:
(add as many lines as characters/narrators)

_____   _____

_____   _____

_____   _____

Now begin to plan what your characters will "say" to share their story. You can add stage directions (movement of characters) if desired with terms such as *enter stage left, exit stage right, moving closer, slowly, smiling, crying,* and so forth.

Narrator: _____

_____

Voice # ___: _____

_____

Voice # ___: _____

_____

Voice # ___: _____

_____

Voice # ___: _____

_____

EXPLANATION FOR APPLICATION OF READING STRATEGY

Radio Reading

Radio Reading (Artley, 1975) is most effective in groups of four to six people. The main objective for radio reading in the content area is to communicate ideas to listeners. Oral reading has a worthwhile function if used to interpret what the writer says, or feels, to concerned listeners. The rules are simple: the reader reads and the listeners listen. When the reader completes reading, the listeners summarize the material. The listeners discuss what was read. The strength of radio reading lies in the discussion strategy. Vacca and Vacca (1996) suggest that the reader initiate discussion by asking questions of the audience. Student questions may tend to be literal and the teacher could lend some support with preprinted higher-level thinking questions as support models during the introductory stages.

Directions: Use the chart on the following page to keep track of reader participation. Appoint a secretary to record who answered each question.

Before Reading

Form small groups; assign the text selection and the segment of text to be read by each group member. Several minutes are given for rehearsal reading by each group member as well as question preparation for the discussion.

During Reading

The first reader begins Radio Reading. As the reader reads, the listeners listen with their *books closed.* Listeners must pay close attention in order to participate in the discussion to follow.

After Reading

At the conclusion of the first segment, the reader initiates discussion, asks questions, and summarizes the passage. Continue with the reader for the next segment. Each listener takes a turn as reader, repeating the During Reading and After Reading instructions.

MODEL FOR APPLICATION OF READING STRATEGY

Radio Reading

Participation and Summary Sheet

Title _____ **A Place Called Freedom** _____, by Scott Russell Sanders

Student	Reader/Questions Answered by . . .					
	#1	**#2**	**#3**	**#4**	**#5**	**Summary**
Sammy	Reader					(see below)
	–	+	+	–	+	+
Jack		Reader				
	+	+	+	+	+	+
Maria			Reader			
	–	+	–	–	+	+
Jody				Reader		
	+	+	–	+	+	+
Michael					Reader	
	+	–	+	+	+	+

Summary

Reader 1 *In 1842 this enslaved family of four was given their freedom by the plantation owner.*

Reader 2 *Following the drinking gourd, the Starman family traveled by night for safety, always heading north.*

Reader 3 *Once in Indiana, a Quaker family helped them farm, earn money, and buy their own land. The Starman family worked hard and wanted to help others.*

Reader 4 *Papa returned to Tennessee many times leading cousins and friends to freedom in Indiana.*

Reader 5 *Hearing of the settlement, black people came from all parts of the South, naming the town Freedom. An educated young James became a teacher and a writer.*

Radio Reading

Participation and Summary Sheet

Title _____

Student	Reader/Questions					
	#1	**#2**	**#3**	**#4**	**#5**	**Summary**
	Reader					
		Reader				
			Reader			
				Reader		
					Reader	

Summary

Reader 1 _____
_____

Reader 2 _____
_____

Reader 3 _____
_____

Reader 4 _____
_____

Reader 5 _____
_____

CHAPTER SIX

Writing to Learn

Writing to Learn Strategies

Notetaking
Double-Entry Journal

Summarizing
Four-Step Summary
Critical Thinking Summary
GRASP the Headings
Incomplete Frames
GIST

Responding
RAFT
Text Talk
Response Journal

ngaging students in different modes of discourse when responding to literature or using content reading materials is important to student growth (Britton et al., 1975; Rosenblatt, 1978; Tompkins, 1997). Incorporating writing with reading and speaking, addresses the informative as well as the creative areas of literacy. Teachers must model writing as a process and provide time for student practice

(Graves, 1983). Through content area writing, students further clarify and extend meaning (Manning & Manning, 1995; Richek et al., 2002).

Research Preview

Research since the 1970s (Tierney & Shanahan, 1991) has investigated the relationship between reading and writing. They have concluded that good writers are often good readers, and good readers are often good writers. Those who write well generally read more; therefore extensive reading improves writing. Students who read and write well perceive themselves as being good at both and therefore engage in the processes independently. By composing through their reading and writing, students construct meaning and elaborate on what they are learning (Tierney & Pearson, 1983).

English Language Arts Standard
Students employ a wide range of strategies as they write and use different writing process elements appropriately to communicate with different audiences for a variety of purposes. Students adjust their use of spoken, written, and visual language (e.g., conventions, style, vocabulary) to communicate effectively (NCTE/IRA, 1996, p. 3).

Connections to Research

If they want students to read and write in the subject area(s) that they teach, content area teachers must be knowledgeable about language as it relates to their field (Howie, 1984). There are some assumptions that they need to have with respect to teaching writing. First they must be cognizant of the fact that all teachers share the responsibility for teaching reading and writing. They need to recognize that knowledge of their subject area helps them to communicate orally and in writing. The use of a social studies text dealing with narration differs from the procedural approach in industrial arts. The more teachers become aware of which mode of operation to use with their subject matter, the greater the understanding the students will have in that content area. Students need to understand that writing is a process that involves prewriting activities, which not only help them research information, but also get them interested in what they want to write and how they want to present it.

Another assumption is that writing is discovery, for it involves the development of ideas through the thinking process. One other assumption is that writing helps to develop maturity. Learning to communicate to different audiences is vital, and using writing—with its organization, structure, and style—generates understanding that writing is much more than merely talk written down. Still another assumption is that students must be taught how to edit what they write. The writer needs to rethink what he or she hopes to communicate so that the content is crystal clear to the reader. Finally, the last assumption is that every teacher can develop a well-planned writing curriculum. We suggest that if teachers utilize the learning strategies outlined in this chapter—which is about "Reading to Write, Writing to Read"—they will assist students in learning the content they are teaching and help them remember what they have learned.

Atwell (1990) agreed with Howie (1984) that teachers of every discipline need to be responsible for teaching writing. Content area teachers must engage students in thinking and writing as historians, mathematicians, scientists, and literary critics. When students as writers assume various roles that are related to their content area reading, they not only learn the information required in that subject but also have a clearer understanding through this process. They truly write to learn.

When students summarize what they have read, they are more likely to understand the content clearly and can then explain it to others through classroom discourse. Writing is basically a process and consists of five parts that seem to occur simultaneously. The parts according to Murray (1987) are highlighted below:

- Collecting information
- Focusing on the most meaningful information

- Ordering or creating structure for our ideas
- Developing what we have to say by talking to ourselves as we write
- Clarifying or polishing what we have written

This writing process requires continuous thinking as students engage in each section outlined above. This thinking is what clarifies understanding of the topic studied in ways that extend learning and lead to further elaboration of ideas. This writing process is not linear, however, but recursive. The writer goes back and forth as he or she learns through this interactive experience.

As students are introduced to new information through lectures, reading, or direct experiences, they are given opportunities to respond in "expressive" writing (Bechtel, 1985), as the process was coined by the Brittish. This means that they can express what they have considered rather than communicating what they definitely know through summaries, questions, comments, or associations. When students know they will freely respond to new information through writing, they are more likely to pay better attention and make connections while they read or listen as well as make connections with what they already know. In addition, the act of writing reinforces memory. This approach helps them extend their learning beyond literal comprehension into the realm of higher-level cognition processes including synthesis, analysis, and evaluation. Students are definitely writing in order to learn, not just to indicate what they know.

According to Vacca and Vacca (1999), there is a very important reason for connecting reading and writing in the content areas. Specifically stated, "When reading and writing are taught in tandem, the union influences content learning in ways not possible when students read without writing or write without reading" (p. 256). When students write about what they have read, they not only think about what they have read, but also they think more deeply about the content. They sometimes develop additional questions that can be further researched or brought out through subsequent classroom discussions. Students write first to clarify their understanding of the text, but then write to make sure that their understandings are communicated clearly to others.

More literature supports the need to write in order to learn in content areas such as science, social science, or math rather than just language arts (Andrews, 1997). Writing gives students a format to demonstrate their understanding of the content. Through writing, they use metacognition to think about their learning and are able to reflect on their understandings in the content areas. In addition, they are able to bridge the gap between new learning and prior knowledge by summarizing the subject area material. The National Reading Panel (2000) emphasized that text comprehension improves when readers are taught to integrate ideas and generalize text information. This is easily accomplished through written summarization.

The **Double-Entry Journal** (Noden & Vacca, 1994; Santa et al., 2004) is an adaptation of a response journal. In the first column of the journal, the student writes down specific information from the text. This may include a word, quote, or passage taken directly from the text, or specific information may be paraphrased by the student. In the second column, the student then writes a reflection on the information recorded in the first column. In summary, the first column can be conceived as a question, "What is it?" while the second column addresses, "What does it mean to you?" This strategy enhances comprehension through writing. It is especially useful with content areas such as social science and science as well as language arts.

The **Four-Step Summary** (Stanfill, 1978; Santa et al., 2004) is one strategy that students can use in any content area whether it be language arts, math, science, social studies, fine arts, physical education, or health. This summary begins by using a four-step formula, which includes identifying the topic, explaining how the reading passage begins, and presenting the ideas in the middle as well as the closing. At least one sentence related to each step should be written in a designated four-column chart. After filling in the information, students write a final summary. The students can work on the Four-Step Summary with the teacher, in a group or partnership, or individually. Going through this process definitely clarifies their understanding of the reading passage, particularly when they create the final summary.

A **Critical Thinking Summary** is useful with any content area, but is especially appropriate for middle and high school students. This strategy helps students to recall information that they have read. The summary requires students to address the following areas related to their reading of content materials in an eight-box format: topic, main idea, thesis, audience, organizational pattern, significance of the thesis or main idea, objective language, subjective language, philosophy, and alternative title. This reflection on what students have read helps them to remember the information.

The **GRASP** (Hayes, 1989) modified as **Grasp the Headings** (Frank, 2001) identifies a guided reading and summarizing procedure. After previewing the titles, pictures, and questions in a passage, the students develop headings that they think refer to the passage. They then write an educated guess related to each heading. Following this process, pupils read the actual passage and then review their responses with a partner. The students then reread the material and add any additional details about each heading. They create a summary paragraph about the story or subject. This is a strategy to use with difficult content materials. By predict-

ing, reading, writing, rereading, writing, and summarizing with a final paragraph, the students are more likely to remember difficult concepts. This is a great strategy for literature, science, and social science texts.

The **Incomplete Paragraph Frame** (Santa et al., 2004; Armbruster et al., 1989) helps students write good paragraphs. This strategy is useful in developing understandings in any content area. The teacher introduces a number of frames that may assist students in learning the organizational patterns of text, learning to identify problem/solution, compare/contrast, cause/effect, sequential, or descriptive text. The students complete a frame, review their written summary with a partner, and then verify the information with the class. Students use the frames to learn about text structure; review material they have read; guide their note taking; and develop skills in answering essay-type questions, in character analysis, and for summarizing reading.

GIST is a strategy (Cunningham, 1982) used to develop the main idea or draw conclusions regarding a reading passage. Students are able to see the big picture of what they are reading by developing a summary. The students consolidate their thoughts alone or with a partner and write a sentence or two about the passage using 20 words or less. The teacher may pose a question that the students need to address related to their reading. For example, in science, the students may be asked to answer the question, "What is Static Electricity?" They would then succinctly respond by filling in no more than 20 blanks outlined on their paper. Their response may read <u>Gaining</u> <u>or</u> <u>losing</u> <u>negative</u> <u>charges</u> <u>causes</u> <u>an</u> <u>electric</u> <u>charge.</u> <u>Charged</u> <u>objects</u> <u>interact,</u> <u>while</u> <u>like</u> <u>objects</u> <u>repel,</u> <u>and</u> <u>unlike</u> <u>charges</u> <u>attract.</u> The students get the gist!

The writing strategy, **RAFT** (Holston & Santa, 1985; Buehl, 2003; Santa et al., 2004), refers to the *R*ole of the writer, the *A*udience, the *F*ormat, and the *T*opic. Students can write about any topic covered in math, science, social studies, even current events. The class is assigned a specific role as the writer, such as consumer, citizen, or soldier. Their audience may be the public, the legislature, or themselves. The format assigned may incorporate writing a letter to the editor, an article for the newspaper, or creating an entry in a diary. A strong verb should be used to stress the importance of describing various effects or explain the reason behind an issue. The important point to make is that the teacher specifies the structure for this writing in advance. This motivational strategy creates interest as students engage in learning about the topic.

Text Talk modeled by Frank (2000) is a strategy involving the interactive responses that students have to the text they are responsible for reading and understanding. Students work with a partner as they read the assigned content area materials. One student poses a question about the material after previewing a specific set of pages, and the other student responds in writing to the question. The process continues—each student posing a question and the partner responding—until the beginning selection has been read. At no time during this process is there oral discourse. Following this silent interactive response time, the teacher asks the class as a whole to present verbally the questions and answers that were generated by the pairs of students. This process works well for language arts, science, and social studies. It is also effective with fine arts and foreign language.

In a **Response Journal** (Hancock, 1993; Richek et al., 2002), students write freely about books that they are reading or topics of class discussion. Journaling gives individuals an opportunity to record their thoughts, reactions, or feelings. The teacher can view their thinking related to the reading assignment or class activities. Sometimes the teacher provides written dialogue with the students through their Response Journals. This can be used to clarify their thought processes or extend thinking. The teacher may also provide prompts related to assignments to emphasize the concepts or details associated with the reading. For example, the student may be expected to fill in the blank from the prompted material supplied by the teacher, such as the date of a specific event; the name of a particular person, place, or thing; and the steps of a math problem, experiment, or recipe. This information is listed in the left-hand column with space on the right for students to indicate what the material means to them. Journals always give students time to reflect on their learning. It is a good strategy to use with language arts, math, science, social studies, fine arts, physical education, and health.

Writing to learn strategies are highly effective when combined with content area reading. Teachers create a climate for constant reflection that increases student understanding of topics and concepts studied in all subject areas. The repetitive reflection provided by teachers across subjects and grade levels ensures that *all* students will automatically use these learning strategies independently. Teaching both reading and writing in all content areas ensures instructional efficiency and student achievement (Shanahan, 1990).

Double-Entry Journal

A Double-Entry Journal (Noden & Vacca, 1994; Santa et al., 2004) is a type of reading/learning log in which the pages are divided into two columns. In the left column, students write notes, quotes, outlines, or calculations of math problems presented in either fiction or nonfiction text. In the right column, students reflect on the information gleaned from the story or informational book. These written reflections can take various forms. For example, if the student recorded a quote from his reading, the reflection can relate the quote to his personal life, the community, or other text he has read. Other "reflections" can be a question, a general reaction, or an explanation of how to do a particular type of math problem.

Before Reading

As a prereading activity, the students can look at pictures and captions relevant to the topic. In addition, they can read headings, introductions, summaries, and end questions. Review with the students how to take their notes, quotes, outlines, and so on.

Demonstrate the format that is needed for the left column. Next, model how to reflect in the right column on the book notes in the left column.

During Reading

As students are reading, ask them to read and record notes, quotations, outlines, diagrams, solutions to math problems, or questions they need clarified.

After Reading

After reading, ask the students to write their reflections to the text notes. Once the students have completed taking the assigned format of notes and the assigned type of reflections, have them write a summary of their Double-Entry Journal. This can take the form of "What I have learned about life." Or, it can be "What the information has to do with my life." It can be a paragraph that answers any question about how the text and the personal reflections relate to the student's life, to another text, or to the world.

Double-Entry Journal

Quotes	Reflections
Chapter 1 _That old van parked with its wheels turned the wrong way was creeping down to the steeper part of the street every time a car went by._	I remember when my niece tried to drive my aunt's car, and the car rolled down the driveway into a car parked on the street.
Chapter 2 _The tone of Tom's voice convinced the police operator that Tom was serious because she immediately sent a squad car to the site._	I know that the police dispatchers always send a squad car when someone calls needing help.

Math Problems $-24 \div 6 = -4$ $-24/6 = -4$	**Explanation of How You Arrived at Your Answer** Divide –24 by 6 and the quotient equals –4. When you divide one negative number by a positive number, the answer requires a negative sign.

Notes from the Book	**Class Discussion**
What makes an airplane stay up? 1. _Top of wing is arched._ 2. _Bottom of wing is flat._ 3. _Faster movement on top of wing reduces pressure on the top._ 4. _Upward push is called "lift."_ _What makes an airplane move?_ 1. _The motor_ 2. _The jet moving air backward forces plane forward_ 3. _Forward force pulls plane along at high speed_	Videos were shown illustrating how the arched wing moves the air faster than the flat bottom. Thus the reduced pressure on the top allows the stronger pressure on the bottom of the wing to push the plane up. The videos showed how the jet engine blades pushed air backwards, forcing the plane forward. The forward force pulled the plane along at high speed.

(continued)

Double-Entry Journal *(continued)*

Question I Had While Reading	Answers from Class Discussion
How can an elephant that is injured or sick be helped by other elephants?	Elephants live in extended families. The two largest elephants in the group take their places on either side of the injured elephant. One pushes up against him. They wrap their trunks around his head, and they push up under his head with their tusks. This way the disabled elephant and the helpers can walk away.

Double-Entry Journal

Notes	Reflections

EXPLANATION OF READING STRATEGY

The Four-Step Summary

This strategy involves creating a summary of text consisting of four sentences. Students practice reducing text into the most important information. Students write to learn, record important data, and apply what they learned. The key to this cognitive-organizing process is the four-step formula (Stanfill, 1978):

1. Identify the topic to be summarized.
2. Tell how the passage begins.
3. Tell what is covered in the middle (main idea and two supporting details).
4. Tell how the passage ends.

Before Reading

Introduce and preview the text to be read. The teacher gives students the Four-Step Summary and discusses the steps in the strategy.

During Reading

The selection is read individually, in pairs, or in small groups.

Students read, keeping in mind the formula used to summarize when finished.

After Reading

After reading, the teacher models the strategy, putting information on the graphic organizer according to the four steps. Use transitions and verbs to connect information. Complete the summary in four sentences, one from each category.

MODEL OF READING STRATEGY

The Four-Step Summary

Steps in Writing a Summary Formula

What are you summarizing?	What does it begin with?	What is in the middle?	How does it end?
Civil Rights Movement	1955 Rosa Parks refused to give her seat on a city bus to a white man.	Laws barred whites and blacks from attending the same schools. Martin Luther King, Jr. believed in nonviolent protest and organized the Montgomery Bus Boycott, which lasted one year. 1960 four African American college students sat at the whites-only counter at Woolworths in Greensboro, NC. 1961 nonviolent Freedom Riders. 1963 Martin Luther King, Jr. led segregation march on Birmingham, AL. 1963 Washington, DC speech by Martin Luther King, Jr. "I have a dream. . . ."	1954 Supreme Court outlawed school segregation by race. 1956 Supreme Court ruled it illegal to have separate seats for African Americans and whites. Within six months, stores agreed to serve food to African American customers. U.S. government ordered an end to whites-only sections in airports, bus and train terminals. 1964 Congress passed the Civil Rights Act.

(continued)

The Four-Step Summary *(continued)*

Final Summary:

The Civil Rights Movement began in the early 1950s through mid-1960s with protests over segregation

laws regarding schools, busses, lunch counters, restrooms and separate waiting areas in airports, bus and

train stations ending with the 1964 congressional Civil Rights Act.

Directions: Fill in the above columns with information from your reading. As you fill in the columns, remember to delete trivial material, delete repetitive material, and provide a term that labels or categorizes a list of items or actions.

Once you have filled in the columns, write a summary sentence using the information for each column. After writing your summary, ask yourself the following questions:

Is anything important left out?

Is the information in the right order?

Have I selected the most important information?

Finally, consider your style of writing. Read each sentence aloud to be sure it reads smoothly: Does it flow easily? Can you change words to smooth it out? Have you used unnecessary words?

Once you have completed all these steps, you probably have written a good four-step summary.

The Four-Step Summary

What are you summarizing?	What does it begin with?	What is in the middle?	How does it end?
Summary Sentence:	**Summary Sentence:**	**Summary Sentence:** (Words and phrases such as *covers, discusses, presents,* and *develops the idea that,* are useful here.)	**Summary Sentence:** (Include *ends with.*)

Final Summary: _____

_____

_____

_____

Critical Thinking Summary

This strategy is appropriate for middle school or older students, but is adaptable for elementary students. Critically thinking about text fosters the movement of students to deeper levels of understanding.

The following terms guide students' critical thinking processes:

Topic is the subject and answers the question, "What is this about?" It usually includes one to three words.

Main Idea includes the topic and answers the question, "What about the topic?" It is in the form of a sentence.

Thesis answers the question, "What does the author want me to do, think, believe, or feel?"

Audience refers to the group of people who will be interested in reading a particular text.

Organizational Pattern is usually one of the following: sequence, examples, reasons, compare/contrast, cause/effect, problem/solution, or opinion/proof.

Significance of the thesis or main idea relates the importance, gravity, or consequence of the thesis or main idea to the reader's life.

Objective Language uses non-emotionally laden words; words that do not carry connotative meanings, but instead are denotative words.

Subjective Language uses emotionally laden words; words that do carry connotative meanings.

Philosophy is the author's systematic view or logical concept about the topic and main idea.

Alternative Title is a creative attempt to use the main idea, the thesis, the organizational pattern, and objective or subjective language to write a different but appropriate title for the text.

The teacher models these terms on a simple piece of text, so that all the students know the definitions and have a set of examples. From the final responses, the teacher models writing the Critical Thinking Summary.

Before Reading

Introduce the above terms and their targeted definitions. Introduce the graphic organizer, which can be used in several ways: as is, or cut apart on the solid lines and each piece glued on a 3×5 note card so that each term is on a separate card. Place the answers on the reverse of the corresponding cards.

During Reading

A student reads the text or article independently answering the four even-numbered questions. A partner reads and answers the four odd-numbered questions.

After Reading

The pair shares and discusses the answers to the eight questions. After answering all the questions, two companion groups come together to share and collaborate on their answers. The teacher then records agreed upon responses on an overhead transparency. At this point, the teacher models writing the Critical Thinking Summary; gradually, students learn to write the summary independently.

Procedure:

- What does the author want you (the particular audience) to know?

- This response covers the questions on main idea, thesis, audience, alternative title, and philosophy.

- What are the supporting categories of information?

- How are the categories organized and how is the article worded (subjective/objective)? This response covers the questions on organizational patterns, and objective and subjective language.

- What importance or consequence does this information have on your life? This covers the question on the significance of the thesis or main idea.

Critical Thinking Summary

Assigned Reading _Silent Spring by Rachel Carson_ **Date** _____

Team Members: _Shawn and Ryan_

1. What is the **topic?** (4 or 5 words) _indiscriminate spraying of sage lands_ What is the **main idea** of the reading? _indiscriminate spraying of sage lands has unexpected consequences._	2. What is the **thesis?** _The indiscriminate spraying of sage lands has resulted in destroying willows along with the sage, creating an imbalance in nature where a chain of events destroyed wildlife and recreation areas._
3. For what **audience** is the author writing? _environmentalists; those with concern for nature_	4. Cite examples from the reading that demonstrated the **organizational pattern.** _cause/effect_
5. Discuss the **significance** of this thesis to your life. _Pesticide spraying over large areas frequently destroys plants other than those intended, resulting in a change in the area's environment._	6. Cite some of the **objective** or **subjective** language the author uses. _Objective:_ _killed sage killed willows lakes drained_ _Subjective:_ _trout may not survive destroys_ _imbalance in nature_
7. What is the author's **philosophy** concerning the topic of the reading? _The author feels that indiscriminate spraying of pesticides is killing wildlife and totally changing the ecosystems in the sprayed areas._	8. Suggest an **alternative title** for the article that is appropriate to the thesis. _Spraying of Pesticides Promotes Changing Ecosystems_

Creating the Summary from the Assigned Reading

Paragraph Beginning

What does the author want you (the particular audience) to know?

This response covers the questions on main idea, thesis, audience, alternative title, and philosophy.

Paragraph Middle

What are the supporting categories of information?

How are the categories organized and how is the article worded (subjective/objective)?

This response covers the questions on organizational patterns, and objective and subjective language.

Paragraph End

What importance or consequence does this information have on your life?

This covers the question on the significance of the thesis or main idea.

The indiscriminate spraying of sage lands creates an imbalance in nature and a change in the ecosystem. A chain of events causes the unexpected results of destroying wildlife like sage and willows and recreational areas. The spraying of pesticides over large areas of land can destroy plants and animals that are not the intended target. This is a drastic and possibly unwanted change in the area's environment.

TEMPLATE OF READING STRATEGY

Critical Thinking Summary

Assigned Reading _____   **Date** _____

Team Members: _____

1. What is the **topic?** (1–3 words) What is the main idea of the reading?	2. What is the **thesis?**
3. For what **audience** is the author writing?	4. Cite examples from the reading that demonstrated the **organizational pattern.**
5. Discuss the **significance** of this thesis to your life.	6. Cite some of the **objective** or **subjective** language the author uses. Objective: Subjective:
7. What is the author's **philosophy** concerning the topic of the reading?	8. Suggest an **alternative title** for the article that is appropriate to the thesis.

GRASP the Headings

Guided Reading and Summarizing Procedure

The GRASP (Hayes, 1989) is a reading strategy that allows the students to use headings to motivate their prior knowledge, to read a passage once and see how much they can remember, and then to do a second reading to fill in any missing information. The final step involves writing a summary paragraph. This modified GRASP the Headings strategy (Frank, 2001) focuses on the value of repeated reading in order to gain full comprehension. Can students "grasp" the concepts of a story, article, or chapter in one reading? This strategy can help students gain insight into their ability to recall facts and ideas. Using the graphic organizer, the teacher walks the students through the summary-writing process.

Before Reading

Students preview titles, subtitles, pictures, and questions. Under each heading, they write down what they think will be in that section. If there are no headings, the teacher turns main ideas into headings for the organizer. The students turn over the paper with the headings and guesses.

During Reading

Students then read the text passage or short story and upon completion, turn the book face down. They then take out the paper with the headings and fill in everything that was important from the passage. They share what they have recorded with a partner, adding any additional information. Then students are asked to open their books, re-read the passage, and record any important ideas omitted from the main concepts.

After Reading

The students share their information with their partners. They then write a summary sentence for each of the headings.

The categories and the information listed become the basis for writing the summary. Write a summary sentence for each of the headings. Be sure to order the sentences. You now have a summary paragraph for the entire reading.

GRASP the Headings

The Rosetta Stone

Importance

key to language of Egypt

3 languages, same inscription

Discovery

1799 found by French officer

found near Alexandria, Egypt

Description

about 3' by 4'

11" thick

Decipherment

Champollion's knowledge of Coptic
  helped recognize Egyptian words.
Studied position and repetition of
  proper names to decode.

Result

Champollion published a
  pamphlet sharing the code.
Scholars unlocked
  literature of ancient Egypt.

The Rosetta Stone

The Rosetta Stone gave the world the key to the long-forgotten language of ancient Egypt. A French officer of Napoleon's engineering corps discovered it in 1799. He found the stone half buried in the mud near Rosetta, a city near Alexandria, Egypt. The Rosetta Stone was later taken to England, where it is still preserved in the British Museum.

On the stone is carved a decree by Egyptian priests to commemorate the crowning of Ptolemy V Epiphanes, King of Egypt from 203 to 181 BC. The first inscription is ancient Egyptian hieroglyphics. The second is in Demotic, the popular language of Egypt at the time. At the bottom of the stone, the same message is written again in Greek.

The stone is made of black basalt, 11 inches thick. It is about 3 feet 9 inches high and 2 feet 4 inches across. Part of the top and a section of the right side of the Rosetta Stone are missing.

The language of ancient Egypt had been a riddle to scholars for many hundreds of years. The Rosetta Stone solved the riddle. A French scholar named Jean Francois Champollion studied the stone. Using the Greek text as a guide, he studied the position and repetition of proper names in the Greek text and was able to pick out the same names in the Egyptian text. This enabled him to learn the sounds of many of the Egyptian hieroglyphic characters.

Champollion had a thorough knowledge of Coptic, the last stage of the Egyptian language that was written mainly with Greek letters. This knowledge enabled him to recognize the meanings of many Egyptian words in the upper part of the inscription. After much work, Champollion could read the entire text. In 1822, Champollion published a pamphlet, *Lettre a M. Dacier*, containing the results of his work. This pamphlet enabled scholars to read the literature of ancient Egypt.

Source: World Book Encyclopedia (1973).

GRASP the Headings

_____   _____   _____
        (Topic)   (Topic)   (Topic)

_____   _____
        (Topic)   (Topic)

Title: _____

       (insert reading or use entire page for recording important information)

Using the individual titles, create a summary of each title and then a summary of the entire reading.

EXPLANATION OF READING STRATEGY

Incomplete Paragraph Frame

Incomplete Paragraph Frames (Santa et al., 2004; Armbruster et al., 1989) can be used with any content area text. This strategy is an excellent way to teach students about organizational patterns of text, by identifying and using problem/solution, compare/contrast, cause/effect, sequential, or descriptive text. Once teachers provide students with cues on textual organization, students are guided to use the writing frames that are appropriate to the material being studied. Frames can be used in a variety of ways: to learn about text structure, to review the material read, to guide note taking, to develop skills in answering essay-type questions, to develop a character analysis, as well as to simply summarize the reading. The teacher can choose to develop his or her personalized frames or use one of those included here. This strategy supports the writing of well-formed paragraphs.

Before Reading

Introduce the material to be read by previewing all headings, pictures, and questions. Review cues to text organization:

Problem/solution: therefore, as a result,

Compare/contrast: similarly, likewise, but, yet, however, on the contrary

Sequence: then, next, first, second, finally, lastly

Cause/effect: because of, causes, therefore, finally, as a result

Descriptive: to begin with, also, most important, in fact

During Reading

Students then read the selection and reflect on the organizational pattern of the text. Determine as a class, the appropriate note-taking graphic and frame for the material being studied.

After Reading

Students reflect on the material read and determine the best phrasing to include in the Incomplete Paragraph Frame. Transition words are substituted or changed to meet the needs of the writer. Writers share their frames with a partner and then share with the class.

MODEL / TEMPLATE OF READING STRATEGY

Incomplete Paragraph Frame

Problem/Solution Text Structure

General Frame: The author is showing the development of a problem and the resulting solution(s).

```
            ┌─────────────────────────────────┐
            │    The problem and the owner     │
            └─────────────────────────────────┘
                            ↓
┌─────────────────────────────┬─────────────────────────────┐
│  Action to solve the problem │     Result of the action    │
└─────────────────────────────┴─────────────────────────────┘
                            ↓
            ┌─────────────────────────────────┐
            │           End result             │
            └─────────────────────────────────┘
```

> *Key Words:*
> therefore
> because
> since
> as a result
> this led to
> thus

Summary Pattern:

_____ had a problem because

_____. Therefore, _____

_____. As a result, _____

_____.

Incomplete Paragraph Frame

Sequential Text Structure

General Frame: The author is putting facts, events, or concepts into an identifiable sequence.

```
┌─────────────────────────────────┐
│  Event 1                        │
└─────────────────────────────────┘
              ↓
┌─────────────────────────────────┐
│  Event 2                        │
└─────────────────────────────────┘
              ↓
┌─────────────────────────────────┐
│  Event 3                        │
└─────────────────────────────────┘
```

Key Words:
first   second
then   next
finally   lastly
before
not long after

Summary Pattern:

Here is how _____ is

made/occurs. First, _____. Next,

_____. Then _____.

Finally, _____.

MODEL/TEMPLATE OF READING STRATEGY

Incomplete Paragraph Frame

Cause/Effect Text Structure

General Frame: The author is showing how concepts, facts, or events happen because of other concepts, facts, or events.

Cause		Cause	

Effect

Key Words:
because of
therefore
causes
as a result

Summary Pattern:

Because of _____, _____,

_____ causes _____.

Therefore _____. Finally, due to

_____, _____.

This explains why _____.

MODEL/TEMPLATE OF READING STRATEGY

Incomplete Paragraph Frame

Compare/Contrast Text Structure

General Frame: The author is pointing out likenesses and differences in concepts, facts, or events.

Concept A

Concept B

> *Key Words:*
> as well as   although
> similarly   likewise
> but   yet
> however   on the contrary
> while

Summary Pattern:

Comparison

_____ and _____ are similar in several ways.

Both _____ and _____,

_____. _____ and

_____ have similar _____.

Finally, both _____ and _____ _____.

Contrast

_____ and _____ are different in several ways.

First of all, _____, while _____. Secondly,

_____ but _____, In addition,

while _____, _____. Finally,

_____ _____, while _____.

Incomplete Paragraph Frame

Descriptive Text Structure

General Frame: The author is connecting ideas through listing important characteristics or attributes of the topic.

Topic

Attribute

Attribute

Key Words:
to begin with
also
most important
in fact
for example

Summary Pattern:

To begin with, _____.

Most important _____, also,

_____. In fact, _____.

For example, _____.

GIST

This strategy (Cunningham, 1982) is great for drawing conclusions and getting to the big picture, the main idea, in any subject area. With practice, students can learn to focus on the core of what they are reading. Younger students may need many rehearsals before they can collapse ideas into one. Sometimes the teacher may want to use this strategy to summarize chapters in a novel unit in order to give the overall picture.

Before Reading

Introduce the material by previewing all headings, pictures, and questions. The teacher explains that the "gist" of something is the main idea. The teacher shares the 20 word-size blanks on an overhead transparency and explains to the students that after reading, they will try to write a sentence or two using 20 words that capture the "gist."

During Reading

Students then read the selection and reflect on words to express the main idea. Students may brainstorm ideas as the reading progresses. Read a page or section, then relate the main idea using only 20 words. Students continue the process, redoing the 20-word summary to include new information.

After Reading

Occasionally, teachers may prefer students consider their thoughts upon completion of the reading. Students can take turns stating their thoughts on the main idea as the teacher records the ideas on the overhead transparency. Each student must continually revise in order to maintain the 20-word allotment.

Students work in pairs to complete the Gist, and then share their product with another pair. Revisions and collaboration on the main idea may be shared, then presented to the entire class. The class can then agree on a main idea summary for the selection.

GIST

Example 1:

What Is Static Electricity?

<u>Gaining</u>   <u>or</u>   <u>losing</u>   <u>negative</u>   <u>charges</u>   <u>causes</u>

<u>electric</u>   <u>charge</u>   <u>or</u>   <u>electric</u>   <u>field.</u>   <u>Charged</u>

<u>objects</u>   <u>interact.</u>   <u>Like</u>   <u>charges</u>   <u>repel,</u>   <u>unlike</u>

<u>charges</u>   <u>attract.</u>

Example 2:

What Is Electric Current?

<u>Electric</u>   <u>current,</u>   <u>a</u>   <u>flow</u>   <u>of</u>   <u>charges</u>

<u>through</u>   <u>a</u>   <u>circuit.</u>   <u>One</u>   <u>path</u>   <u>for</u>

<u>current</u>   <u>is</u>   <u>series</u>   <u>circuit,</u>   <u>more</u>   <u>than</u>

<u>one,</u>   <u>parallel.</u>

GIST

A Summary of Twenty Words or Less

After reading the passage, write a sentence or two of no more than 20 words that capture the "gist" of what you read. Use the 20 word-size blanks.

_____ _____ _____ _____

_____ _____ _____ _____

_____ _____ _____ _____

_____ _____ _____ _____

_____ _____ _____ _____

With the people at your table, or your partner, consolidate your ideas on what the "gist" of the passage is, and then record the agreed upon consensus in a one or two sentence summary of no more than 20 words. Use the 20 word-size blanks.

_____ _____ _____ _____

_____ _____ _____ _____

_____ _____ _____ _____

_____ _____ _____ _____

RAFT

The RAFT technique (Holston & Santa, 1985) empowers students with a meaningful avenue to incorporate writing into content area instruction. RAFT is especially engaging because students write to an audience other than their teacher, and they write for a specific purpose. Since writing is specific and focused, students better understand the need to explain the topic clearly and completely. This technique can be used with any topic from current events to math. RAFT consists of four major components, namely the following:

Role of the Writer	Who are you?	student, plant, soldier
Audience	To whom is this written?	president, public, self
Format	What form will it take?	letter, article, diary
Topic + Strong Verb	What topic of importance have I chosen?	describe effects of . . . , explain why . . . , warn about

Before Reading

Introduce the material to be read by previewing all topics, pictures, and questions. Brainstorm with students the many varied and possible "points of view" that could be used to relate opinions or feelings about the topic they are about to read. To whom could these be expressed? Record these on the board.

During Reading

Students then read the selection, keeping in mind the viewpoints that others (or objects) could possibly contribute on the subject. A variation is to assign students a point of view and have them use Post-its as they read to mark the information that supports their assigned point of view.

After Reading

Upon completion of the reading, explain that all writers need to consider four components of every composition: the role of the writer, the audience, the format, and the topic. Then, brainstorm additional ideas about the topics that came to mind during the reading. Write RAFT on the board and list possible roles, audiences, formats, and strong verbs that are appropriate for each topic.

Have students choose one example from each category to incorporate into their writing about the topic.

RAFT

Subject _____

Brainstorm options, or consider some of the following:

Role	**A**udience	**F**ormat	**T**opic
colonist	King of England	letter	unfair taxation
student	president	letter	views on foreign policy
columnist Erik Zorn	public	letter to editor	recycling in the city
constituent	U.S. senator	letter	save the swamps
square root	whole number	explain relationship	How does this figure?
motorist	police officer	plea	I don't deserve a ticket because . . .
scientist	Jonas Salk	research brief	vaccinations
monkeys	zookeeper	e-mail	concerns about health
CEO	secretary	memo	cost cutting measures
plant	sun	thank you note	photosynthesis process
mineral	6th grade student	report	our uses and functions
hot dog	bun	dialogue	how to assemble this lunch
student	teacher	research report	circulatory system

RAFT

Subject _____ **Social Studies Activity** _____

My Choices:

Role: Fourth Grade Student

Audience: President of the United States

Format: Letter

Topic: Government

April 7, 2003

1600 Pennsylvania Avenue
Washington, D.C. 20500

Dear Mr. President,

I am Megan. This year in Social Studies I have been learning about the government and how the people vote for Representatives in Congress. I thought it was so interesting to find out how people vote for the Presidents, like you.

I also learned that there are three branches to the Federal Government. The first branch is the Executive and that's what you are. I also learned that you enforce the laws after the Congress makes the laws. I think it's very cool that you are the President and get to live in the White House. Is it hard to take care of everything at once? I sure think it would be for me. What I also think is really cool is the Constitution and the Bill of Rights. Our government has worked well for many years.

I really think that learning about you, what Representatives take care of, and how the Government works is very cool and interesting. I also think that being the President is an AWESOME job to have! I wish you all the best.

Your friend,

Megan

TEMPLATE OF READING STRATEGY

RAFT

Subject _____

My Choices:

Role: _____

Audience: _____

Format: _____

Topic: _____

EXPLANATION OF READING STRATEGY

Text Talk

(Written Conversations)

Text Talk, another name for Written Conversations (Gallagher & Norton, 2000), is an interactive writing experience that takes place in a meaningful social context. Students learn to manipulate language through communication by way of a written exchange of questions and responses related to text. This strategy is appropriate for all ages and is especially useful for reluctant writers.

The rules are simple: No talking! Students carry on the conversation with each other in writing. The text or material is assigned to partners.

Before Reading

Introduce and preview the text to be read. Students preview titles, subtitles, pictures, questions, and summary. As a class, discuss and predict. Each student develops a question they anticipate the text will answer. The papers are exchanged with the partner.

During Reading

Students then read a page or two of the selection and attempt to answer the partner's question. They write a comment or response to the material. Each student then asks a new question. Papers are exchanged and the process continues for about 10 to 15 minutes.

After Reading

Upon completion of the reading, the teacher accepts a question/response sheet from each pair of students. The students independently finish the text.

Text Talk

(Written Conversations)

Partners _____ *Jessica* _____ and _____ *Amy* _____

Topic _____ *The Age of Jefferson* _____ Date _____

- Read a page or section from your textbook.
- Write a question about the reading.
- Trade papers with your partner.
- Answer your partner's question and write a comment.
- Repeat until the assigned reading is complete.

Question: Page # _____

What did Daniel Boone contribute to early exploration in America?

_____

(Trade papers now and answer your partner's question, then make a comment.)

Answer:

In 1775, Daniel Boone and others cut a 300-mile path from eastern Virginia to the Kentucky River, right through

the Appalachian Mountains Cumberland Gap. This path was known as the "Wilderness Trail."

Comment:

Correct

_____

Question: Page # _____

What was the purpose and result of the Lewis and Clark expedition?

(Trade papers now and answer your partner's question, then make a comment.)

Answer:

President Jefferson sought funds for a scientific and geographical expedition to explore lands to the Pacific

Ocean. The explorers kept detailed records of the land, plants, wildlife, and people of the West during their

journey, 1804 to 1806, opening further westward expansion.

Comment:

Correct—What an adventure for that time.

_____

Text Talk

(Written Conversations)

Partners _____ and _____

Topic _____ Date _____

- Read a page or section from your textbook.
- Write a question about the reading.
- Trade papers with your partner.
- Answer your partner's question and write a comment.
- Repeat until the assigned reading is complete.

Question: Page # _____

_____

_____

(Trade papers now and answer your partner's question, then make a comment.)

Answer:

_____

_____

Comment:

_____

_____

Question: Page # _____

_____

(Trade papers now and answer your partner's question, then make a comment.)

Answer:

_____

_____

Comment:

_____

_____

Response Journal

A Response Journal is exactly what the name indicates—a written response to various genre: literature, poetry, mathematics, history, or geography. Brozo (1989) (Richek et al., 2002) describes the Reader Response Journal as a vehicle to provide a personal and meaningful connection to text in order to support retention. A Response Journal allows readers to create a permanent record of what they feel or think as they interact with text. Teachers may prefer to use prompts to jumpstart student thinking or emotional reaction to the subject, especially with the first few attempts. This is not writing for the teacher to score, correct, grade, or criticize. The purpose of student writing in this format is to engage in free writing and free expression as a response to text. Comprehension is enhanced through personalization of thoughts and ideas. A graphic organizer is included, but a spiral notebook with divided pages may work better for some purposes.

Before Reading

Introduce the material to be read by previewing all headings, pictures, and questions. Good readers reflect on what they know and how information may personally affect them.

During Reading

Students read the selection, and record in their Response Journals their thoughts, feelings, opinions, questions, likes, or dislikes connected to the reading.

After Reading

Occasionally, teachers may prefer that students consider their thoughts on the reading upon completion of the reading. Using notes taken during reading can support students as they engage in class discussion, sharing ideas, thoughts, and opinions as well as their interpretations of the facts, events, or ideas presented in the reading.

Student Guidelines for the Response Journal:

Write down everything that you are thinking about while you read. The journal is a way of recording those fleeting thoughts that pass through your mind as you interact with the text.

Don't worry about the accuracy of spelling and mechanics in the journal.

Record the number of the page read, then look back to reread and verify your thoughts.

Write on one side of your graphic organizer or use a spiral notebook.

Relate what you are reading to your own experience.

Ask questions while reading. Question characters' behaviors.

Make predictions about what will happen as the plot unfolds.

Validate or change those predictions as you continue reading the text. Do not worry about being right or wrong.

Praise or criticize the book's author, style, or point of view.

Talk to the characters. Give them advice or put yourself in their place. How would you act in a similar situation?

There is no limit to the type of responses. These guidelines are starters, not limits to the kinds of things you can write.

Response Journal

Name _____

Topic: _Settlers in Jamestown_   **What this means to me . . .**

(Text)	(Response to text)
Every community has a story about how it began. Settlers to Jamestown, Virginia, came across the Atlantic Ocean by ship, from England.	*I wonder how long this voyage took? This seems a bit scary.*
They did not know what to expect as far as their home, the weather, plants that would grow, animals for food, or exactly where they would live.	
The settlers arrived in the spring of 1607. They were rich people who had come to build a colony. A colony is a group of people who settle in a new land.	*I have always lived in the same house. This sounds like going camping.*
The settlers built a fort. Their fort had three wooden walls for protection. It was in the shape of a triangle.	*I have built forts of snow, I thought forts were square or round.*
After the fort was built, instead of hunting, planting, or gathering firewood, many men went bowling. On the days they did not want to bowl, men looked for gold.	*Where in the world would settlers go bowling in the wilderness? I'm sure looking for gold was fun.*
Captain John Smith became the leader of the settlers. He told the settlers they needed to work if they were going to live through the winter.	*Good thing Captain Smith came forward to be the leader.*
Settlers made friends with Chief Powhaten, leader of the Native Americans. Settlers traded metal pots, axes, and knives for corn and tobacco seeds. To trade means to give something to get something.	*With help from the Native Americans, the settlers survived.*

TEMPLATE OF READING STRATEGY

Response Journal

Name _____

Topic of Reading: _____   **What this means to me . . .**

(Text)	(Response to text)

CHAPTER SEVEN

Studying Text

Studying Text Strategies

Questioning

Carousel Brainstorming
Questioning the Text
Question–Answer Relationship
   (Q.A.R.)
Inquiry Chart (I-Chart)

Text Structure
↓
Nonfiction Text
SQ3R
Internal Text Structures & Frames
     Sequence
     Cause/Effect
     Problem/Solution
     Classification/Network
     Descriptive
     Comparison/Contrast

Studying requires hard work, and students need to learn how to engage in the process. They need to realize why they are studying and then address that purpose by acquiring, organizing, summarizing, or using information or ideas (Vacca & Vacca, 2005). They must look for the "structure" of the text, that is, the way the important information is organized in the written material whether it is in a textbook, trade book, reference source, or electronic text. This understanding of the organization is pertinent to both comprehension and retention (Salisbury, 1934; Smith, 1964; Niles, 1965; Herber, 1978). Teachers suggest studying strategies that increase student understanding of content reading materials.

Research Preview
Students must be able to frame questions for inquiry, identify and organize relevant information from a variety of sources (written, visual, and electronic), and communicate it effectively (Illinois State Board of Education, 1997). These study skills are important across all content areas in school, but they are vital to career as well as lifelong learning. Delegating control to students for learning goals, namely self-monitoring, or metacognition to foster independence and achievement leads to effective independent learning (Haller, Child, & Walberg, 1988; Palincsar & Brown, 1984; Pearson, 1985).

English Language Arts Standard
As a result of their schooling, students will be able to read with understanding and fluency. They will also use language arts to acquire, assess, and communicate information (Illinois Learning Standards, 1997, p. 4; p. 12).

Connections to Research

Studying text provides a framework for students to use in processing information and thinking more in depth about ideas encountered in their reading (Vacca & Vacca, 2005). Whether using the internet, referring to trade books, or selecting a novel, students become aware of the genuine use of text. They begin to make connections in their reading, writing, and discussions through text that helps them explore, solve problems, gain information, or be entertained.

Text structure incorporates story structure, as well as an internal or external organization. Story structure incorporates a set of elements (Vacca & Vacca, 1999) that creates a causal chain of events. These elements include the following:

1. *An initiating event:* An idea or action that sets events in motion.
2. *An internal response:* An emotional reaction to the initiating event.
3. *An attempt:* Efforts to solve the problem or achieve a goal.
4. *Consequence:* The success or failure of the attempts to solve the problem.
5. *A resolution:* An action that resolves or does not resolve the problem.
6. *A reaction:* A feeling related to the success or failure of the problem.

Students can use story structure in learning and retaining ideas encountered in reading, particularly in fiction.

External text structure provides features that are organizational aides to facilitate reading. Most books follow a similar format in that they generally include a table of contents, appendixes, a bibliography, and indexes. Each chapter generally includes an introduction, headings, charts, graphs, illustrations, and guide questions. Headings help to divide the text into logical units. This external text structure helps to highlight important ideas. Students need to learn how to utilize external text structure in comprehending content area materials.

Internal text structure generally presents content in a hierarchical relationship. The ideas in the informational text are organized into levels of subordination. The top level includes the most important ideas, the next level supports these ideas, and the bottom level provides the supporting details for each idea. Skilled readers differentiate the important ideas from the unimportant ones. Good readers look for major thought relationships (Meyer, Brandt, & Bluth, 1980). They determine the predominant text pattern that ties the ideas in their assigned text together. Five text patterns seem to be used in written assignments: description, sequence, comparison and contrast, cause and effect, and problem and solution. Teachers need to help all students understand how to use internal text structure to comprehend and retain the material that they are expected to learn.

Students who study effectively recognize the organization of the material. They know how to approach a text assignment, to analyze the reading required, to make plans for reading, and to use those strategies that match the purpose of their study. It is very hard work. Study means that students must be able to retain all of the important ideas encountered in their reading. While they may do this in their heads, there are also frameworks that they can use or study systems that can assist them in learning the information and remembering it. Perceiving the structure of text definitely improves learning and retention. Teachers can help students use organization of text structure as a process for comprehending and retaining the material that they encounter.

All students can learn strategies for studying text whether they are in a language arts, science, social science, mathematics, fine arts, foreign language, physical education, or health class. Some of the strategies that can assist them in not only learning the material but also in remembering it are provided in the following paragraphs.

Carousel Brainstorming is a strategy that Cecilia Frank and Jan Grossi developed to get students to work collaboratively to address a topic of study. The students are given Post-its to use in responding to Anticipation Guide statements that the teacher generated from text. The students mark agree, disagree, or unsure. Each response note is placed on the appropriately prepared statement poster. A team is assigned to each poster to analyze the data, create a bar graph

with the responses, and write a descriptive paragraph. The text is then read and the before-reading steps are repeated. Next teams write a descriptive paragraph as a result of their analysis of the after-reading responses. This leads to further discussion related to the issues addressed in their content area reading. Finally, the class holds a town meeting. They write down a **Think (Things I Now Know)** and a **Wink (What I Need to Know)** to create a chart of questions for further inquiry.

Questioning the Text (Giles, 1987; Buehl, 2003) is a strategy that encourages students to question what they are reading. By asking questions, they can confirm or disprove what they have predicted about the material they read. This is especially helpful when students encounter difficult text. By stopping to question what they are reading, students can make associations with their own experiences and prior learning. The students are actively engaged in the reading process and this helps them not only think about what they are reading but also clarify their understanding of the content presented in the text.

Question–Answer Relationships or **Q.A.R.** (Raphael, 1986) is an excellent strategy to use in studying text. The students can use this the text or knowledge that they have in their heads to address the questions they have with regard to the information they are reading. They can address four categories: First, an answer may be *right there,* and the students can find it in the text they are reading. Second, an answer may require *think and search* in that the answer is in the text, but the students must assimilate it from putting parts of the story together. Thirdly, the students may have to use prior experiences to find it "in their heads" or more appropriately labeled *on my own.* Finally, the students cannot find it in the text, but based on what they know and what has been read, they construct it in their heads through the *author and you.* Knowing where the answers can be found, and then addressing the question definitely helps students in studying text.

Creating an I-Chart (Leu & Leu, 2000; Blachowicz & Ogle, 2001; Buehl, 2003) is a way for students to work individually or with a partner to conduct research by investigating a problem through various resources including the use of the internet. The student(s) create a chart to address self-generated questions that guide their investigation or the speech that they plan to present. They chart where they obtained their information and specific details related to the topic. This chart provides pertinent material that strengthens their investigation and assists them in presenting the information to their particular audience. It is an excellent way to classify and sort various pieces of data. Through the use of the I-Chart, students are able to accurately cite their research and provide the details necessary in speech making or developing research papers.

SQ3R (Robinson, 1946) is a strategy that teachers can use with every content area. It affects what happens before students read, while they are reading, and what they do after reading. The students *survey* the text, make *questions* out of the headings, *read* the material, *record* important information, and *review* the information they have compiled. The students establish a purpose for reading by asking questions and therefore tune in to the material to be studied during reading.

By recording information, they develop a form of note taking, which helps them review the material that they learned to help them remember it.

Internal Text Structure (Meyer & Rice, 1984; Tompkins, 1994; Vacca & Vacca, 2005; Richek et al., 2002) helps the students to recognize the way the author has organized the content and see the hierarchical relationship among the ideas presented in the text. Generally there are five text patterns that are used by the author. These include description, sequence, comparison and contrast, cause and effect, and problem and solution. The students learn to see the pattern and address the appropriate relationship through a specific graphic organizer. The students then generate a summary for whatever pattern is used. By writing down comparison information concerning the content, the students are more capable of comprehending material and remembering the ideas presented in the text. This is helpful in discussing a topic, reflecting on what they have read, or reviewing for a test.

Helping students learn how to study text is vital to success in school. Some children naturally know how to study whereas others need assistance in learning how to do so. The strategies in this chapter are great tools to model and use with students who eventually use them on their own. Studying text improves comprehension and solidifies learning content, especially when summaries are written.

EXPLANATION FOR APPLICATION OF READING STRATEGY

Carousel Brainstorm

Carousel Brainstorm is a strategy that includes the use of several activities that move from one to another, much as a carousel turns. This concept for study engages students in text and is extremely beneficial to students in a diverse classroom. The multiple strategy approach to text insures that each student gains insight and understands textual concepts. The approach is from Cecilia Frank and Jan Grossi.

Before Reading

Each student is given five "Post-it" notes, which are numbered 1–5. On several large poster size sheets of paper, the teacher has written five Anticipation Guide Statements about a topic of study to be reviewed or previewed. Students are asked to respond to each statement and give a brief rationale for each response (Agree, Disagree, or Unsure) on a "Post-It" note. Then they give a brief reason why they responded that way. Students are next invited to place each response note on the appropriate poster-size papers. Next, divide students into five teams. Each team is given one of the statement posters with the task of analyzing the data and making a bar graph using the responses from the "Post-it" notes. Provide each team with an overhead transparency and markers. Have them write a descriptive paragraph about the results from their graphing. Share the descriptive paragraphs with the class.

Open up the group for further discussion of the issues.

This interactive strategy sets the purpose for reading (to gain insight and information about this topic). Preview the text noting headings, pictures, charts, and other information. Look at the end questions to help readers think about why they are reading.

During Reading

Students begin reading the selection. As they come to things they do not understand, students write their questions in the first column of the information organizer. The students read to find answers to their questions.

After Reading

After reading, the students answer their own questions in column two. Distribute five "Post-its." Invite students to again respond to the five Anticipation Guide poster statements. Have original teams produce graphs using the final responses and write a new summary statement. Compare and contrast the pre- and post graphs. Share summary reports in the large group.

Finally, hold a town meeting: Write down a **THINK** (**Th**ing **I** **N**ow **K**now) and a **WINK** (**W**hat **I** **N**eed to **K**now). Record **WINK**s and create a chart of questions for further inquiry.

Carousel Brainstorm Worksheet

Team members _____

Materials: 10 "Post-it" notes per student (5 for prereading, 5 for postreading)
5 jumbo sheets of chart paper for Anticipation Guide Statements
Transparency and markers for each study group (4 students)
Graphic Organizer (supplied below)

Before Reading

- All students place their five Post-it responses on the Anticipation Guide Posters.

- Five teams are formed and each assigned a poster.

- In response to the poster statement, each team creates a bar graph labeled: Agree, Disagree, Unsure.

- Using information from Post-it notes, write a descriptive paragraph as follows:

    First sentence: The majority answered . . .

    Second sentence: The minority stated . . .

    Third sentence: There were _____ True, _____ False, and _____ Unsure.

    Fourth sentence: Most students think that the answer to _____ is _____.

During Reading

Questions I Have	Answers I Can Give
Paragraph One	
Paragraph Two	
Paragraph Three	
Paragraph Four	

After Reading

Using your second "Post-it," revote your answer to the Anticipation Guide Statements. Graph the final responses and write a summary statement that compares and contrasts the information on the two graphs. Share a summary report in the large group.

Descriptive paragraph from "Post-it" notes:

_____

_____

_____

_____

_____

Participate in a town meeting. Write down a **THINK** (**TH**ing **I** **N**ow **K**now) and a **WINK** (**W**hat **I** **N**eed to **K**now). Share responses in large group and create a chart of the questions for further inquiry.

THINK: _____

_____

WINK: _____

_____

EXPLANATION FOR APPLICATION OF READING STRATEGY

Questioning the Text

This strategy, Questioning the Text (Giles, 1987; Buehl, 2003) encourages students to question and engage in active reading of text as well as other reading material. Reading comprehension involves making predictions, asking questions, and then reading to confirm or modify these predictions. When students are confronted with especially difficult material, they stop active reading—that is, they stop questioning and stop making associations with their own lives.

Before Reading

The teacher discusses the reading process with students. Select a difficult passage to read aloud and discuss in order to model how students can ask questions during the reading. Vary the kind of questions you demonstrate. Show students that many of these questions can be answered by simply reading further in the selection. Using the included graphic organizer, note that half of the paper is labeled "Questions I Have," while the other half is labeled "Answers I Can Give." Note the assigned page numbers at the top of the organizer.

During Reading

Students begin reading the selection. As they come to things they do not understand or have questions about, students write down their questions in the first column.

After Reading

After reading the entire selection, students return to their questions. Now that they have more information, the students answer their questions.

Questioning the Text

Assigned Pages: Algebra, Lesson 1: pages 9–18

Questions I Have	Answers I Can Give
Algebra is confusing to me, why are letters and numbers combined to work math problems?	Algebra is a branch of mathematics that denotes quantities with letters and uses negative numbers as well as ordinary numbers.
What are integers?	The integers are all the positive whole numbers, their opposites, and zero.
How could I possibly use algebra in my daily life?	Balancing a checkbook: deposits = positive numbers, while checks and service charges = negative numbers. Profit and loss statements, temperature changes.
In working my problems, how can $-8 - (-2) = -6$? Don't like signs add? How can $7 - (-2) = 9$	In a subtraction problem, $(-)$ is the same as a positive number. so . . . $-8 - (-2) = -8 + 2 = -6$ and . . . $7 - (-2) = 7 + 2 = 9$
Mathematical expressions are so confusing, what does it mean to simplify an expression? Ex: $(3 + 4) \times (2 + 5) = $ I think 49??	There is a specific order you must follow. *Order of Operations:* 1. Perform operations inside grouping symbols. 2. Do all multiplication and division in order from left to right. 3. Do all addition and subtraction in order from left to right. *Using the Order of Operations:* Ex: $3 + 4 \times 2 + 5$ first, add $3 + 4$, next add $2 + 5$ so then . . . 7×7 will then $= 49$

Questioning the Text

Assigned Pages: _____

Questions I Have	Answers I Can Give

EXPLANATION FOR APPLICATION OF READING STRATEGY

Question–Answer Relationships (Q.A.R.)

Taking the time to teach students how to find the answers to questions is a valuable lifetime study tool (Raphael, 1986). Answers to questions can be found in one of two places—in the text or in your head. Many questions are factual in nature and answers are **"Right There,"** stated in the text. Other questions require reading several paragraphs or pages. Students need to think about what they read, and search for information related to the question. Then students need to think about how the relevant information is related to answer the question. This is a **"Think and Search"** question. The answers are in the text but the student must think about the different text parts and put ideas together, creating the answer. Other questions may fall into the "in your head," category. An **"On My Own"** question requires the student to call upon his or her background experiences and knowledge to determine the answer, while **"Author and You"** questions want each student to think about what he or she already knows, what the author says, and how those two pieces fit together. Raphael introduces us to this strategy and the mnemonics for the question-and-answer relationship technique.

Q.A.R. is an excellent strategy to assist in studying text. This strategy also presents an excellent opportunity to begin teaching students how text can work for them. Begin by teaching students to preview the material they are about to read. On each page, point out and discuss all pictures, captions, charts, headings, and any other data but do not read the text at this point. Use the ideas and your logic to produce a poster that students can use as a reference point while becoming familiar with the terms and guidelines for this strategy.

Before Reading

The teacher introduces the concept of Q.A.R. by showing a poster made earlier. (If you would prefer, make an overhead transparency containing the description of each of the four Q.A.R. relationships.) Read over the titles and descriptions for each of the question types from the poster. Preview the chapter's end questions. Use those end questions as the practice model to determine the Q.A.R. category for each question.

During Reading

During reading, the students are aware of questions they are expected to answer or discuss, once they have finished reading. One visual support is to give students small "Post-it" notes to place in their reading to mark the place where each has found the answer. Students then can readily share a **"Right There"** answer or show where **"Think and Search"** information can be located. The teacher knows from spotting the "Post-its" that students have all participated and understood the concept.

After Reading

The teacher reads the first question aloud to the class and students help decide what type of question it represents: **Right There, Think and Search, Author and You,** or **On My Own.** Students may refer to the poster to justify their choices. Discuss why the question was identified as a certain type and then answer the question. Write the answer to the question in a complete sentence.

Go to the remaining questions and move through the above steps with each. Students' understanding of text will deepen and expand.

Practice Locating Answers Using Q.A.R. Strategy

Native Americans and Newcomers

1. Why did settlers build a community in Dubuque?

Q.A.R.:   Right There _____   Author and You _____

                Think and Search _____X_____   On My Own _____

The Mesquakie allowed Dubuque to mine lead from the earth. New settlers came to work in the mines; others came to farm the land.

2. What are some ways that Dubuque changed over the years?

Q.A.R.:   Right There _____X_____   Author and You _____

                Think and Search _____   On My Own _____

Miners needed a place to stay, so hotels were built where meals were served and laundry done, streets lit with gas lights, fire department, public schools, and public market.

3. Why do you think Julian Dubuque and the Mesquakie agreed to work together?

Q.A.R.:   Right There _____X_____   Author and You _____

                Think and Search _____   On My Own _____

They were friends.

4. What are the various ways that the nearby railroad and riverboats changed the Dubuque community?

Q.A.R.:   Right There _____   Author and You _____

                Think and Search ____X_____   On My Own _____

More settlers came to Dubuque.

5. Settlers looked for land that was good for growing crops. What type of land do you have in your area? Dig up some soil. Is it moist, sandy, rocky, dry?

Q.A.R.:   Right There _____   Think and Search _____

                Author and You _____   On My Own _____X_____

Soil in our area is moist and black; consequently it is good for growing crops.

Locating Answers Using Q.A.R. Strategy

1. _____?

Q.A.R.: Right There _____   Author and You _____

Think and Search _____   On My Own _____

_____

_____

2. _____?

Q.A.R.: Right There _____   Author and You _____

Think and Search _____   On My Own _____

_____

_____

3. _____?

Q.A.R.: Right There _____   Author and You _____

Think and Search _____   On My Own _____

_____

_____

4. _____?

Q.A.R.: Right There _____   Author and You _____

Think and Search _____   On My Own _____

_____

_____

5. _____?

Q.A.R.: Right There _____   Author and You _____

Think and Search _____   On My Own _____

_____

_____

EXPLANATION FOR APPLICATION OF READING STRATEGY

I-Chart

Inquiry Research/Investigating the Problem

The I-Chart strategy (Leu & Leu, 2000; Blachowicz & Ogle, 2001; Buehl, 2003) is an excellent tool for students to use when organizing material to write a speech or a research paper. Once the teacher walks students through the steps and the student creates a research paper or speech, the format will forever be a mental guide for students to follow in their pathway of learning.

First the teacher reads a primary source material for inquiry. As students listen to the reading, they form questions or "I wonder . . ." statements (Allen, 2000). These questions or statements become the major components of the investigation.

Before Reading

The teacher discusses the purpose and goal of the proposed inquiry or investigation. The teacher reads the primary source of information to the class. Using a model, the teacher conducts a "think-aloud" demonstrating possible questions or "I wonder . . ." statements. Students collect information from three or more sources as they attempt to answer their research questions.

During Reading

Students begin by skimming and reading the sources. Practice with headings, sub-headings, previewing text strategies. Read the first or last sentence in paragraphs to cue in on the main ideas. As students come to information they could use in their research, it is recorded on the I-Chart (page numbers may be added as the teacher requires).

After Reading

After students have completed the chart, they are ready to summarize their information and compose their paper or speech.

I-Chart

Inquiry Research/Investigating the Problem

Famous Person (Character) Speech

Questions or "I wonder . . ." Statement	Early Life/Family & Childhood	Education	Contributions & Accomplishments	Other Pertinent Information
Resources with Citation				
Encyclopedia				
Online Site				
Book				
Magazine				
Summary				

I-Chart—Guiding Questions

Topic	1.	2.	3.	4.	Interesting Facts & Figures	New Questions
What We Know						
1. Source						
2. Source						
3. Source						
Summary						

EXPLANATION FOR APPLICATION OF READING STRATEGY

SQ3R

Survey, Question, Read, Record, Review

Many students require a systematic approach to studying text, and SQ3R is just that. Francis Robinson created this study strategy in 1946, and it is the cornerstone of modern strategies. This method of study was designed to take advantage of the consistent format in most traditional textbooks. Since each chapter contains a title, introduction, a number of headings and subheadings, a concluding or summary statement, and some questions or problems posed by the textbook authors, the format leads to a five-step study procedure: Survey, Question, Read, Record, and Review. SQ3R incorporates many of the accepted principles of learning—activating prior knowledge, setting a purpose, and constructing meaning.

Survey: Students preview material to anticipate content, make plans for reading, get a sense of the sequence of text, and develop a mental framework for ideas to be encountered in text. There is so much to check out before reading—chapter title, headings, subheadings, words, phrases, special type, pictures, diagrams, illustrations, charts, and graphs.

Question: Students ponder or raise questions from the headings and subheadings.

Read: Students read in search of ideas and information to help answer the questions raised.

Record: Students attempt to answer their questions aloud to rehearse their learned response to questions. Answers may also be written.

Review: Students review and reflect on material by organizing and elaborating on ideas encountered in text and rereading portions to verify or expand on responses to their questions.

Before Reading

The teacher introduces the concept of SQ3R by reviewing the above terms. Before beginning any chapter in a textbook, **survey** it. The teacher asks the students to quickly look over the chapter title, headings or subheadings, the introduction, the chapter summary, and any illustrations, charts, and graphs to get an idea of what the chapter is about.

Question is the step that activates the brain for learning. The students go back to the beginning of the chapter and turn the first heading into a question, so they know what they are trying to find out while reading. For example, if the heading is "the Colonial Period," readers should ask themselves the following **questions:** What is the Colonial Period? When was the Colonial Period? What was important about the Colonial Period? Record these questions on the left-hand side of the graphic organizer (or a piece of paper).

During Reading

During reading, the students **read** the assignment, keeping in mind the questions they have created. The readers **record** notes while reading. The notes answer the readers' self-made questions, which include major

(continued)

SQ3R

Survey, Question, Read, Record, Review *(continued)*

ideas and important details of the chapter. Notes can be done in a variety of formats: outline, Two-Column Notes, Structured Overview, or our graphic organizer. Readers should monitor their reading speeds, and slow down for difficult parts. They will need to stop and reread parts that aren't clear.

important ideas, reviewing the answers to the self-made questions, and reviewing the answers to author-made questions at the end of the chapter. Ideas from discussion and other ideas are added to the notes at this time.

After Reading

The readers review by rereading the structured notes from the chapter, checking for

SQ3R

"A Daily Weather Map Represents the Condition of the Atmosphere"

Before Reading: Survey the title, subtitle, captions, and author-made questions. Make questions out of the subtitles.

During Reading: The reader will record the main ideas supporting details, information from pictures and captions, and answers to self-made questions, as well as author-made questions.

After Reading: The notes are reviewed to make sure all important information has been recorded. Any other information that helps answer key questions can be added at this point.

Heading or Subheading Questions	Answers from Reading Text
How do storms move across the United States?	Storms move from east to west across the United States.

How do high- and low-pressure areas affect weather?	When there is a low-pressure area, the air is moving up.
	When there is a high-pressure area, the air is moving down.
	See Picture in text:
	    Low-Pressure Area : warm, cloudy weather
	    High-Pressure Area: cool, clear weather

How are weather maps created?	Weather stations report daily atmospheric conditions to Washington for creating weather maps.
How is the weather predicted?	Satellites send pictures of the Earth's cloud cover. Computers help forecast the weather.

SQ3R

_____

Title

Before Reading: Survey the title, subtitle, captions, and author-made questions. Make questions out of the subtitles.

During Reading: The reader will record the main ideas supporting details, information from pictures and captions, and answers to self-made questions, as well as author-made questions.

After Reading: The notes are reviewed to make sure all important information has been recorded. Any other information that helps answer key questions can be added at this point.

Heading or Subheading Questions	Answers from Reading Text

EXPLANATION FOR APPLICATION OF READING STRATEGY

Internal Text Structure

This strategy (Armbruster et al., 1989; Tompkins, 1994; Vacca & Vacca, 2005; Richek et al., 2002) tells, shows, describes, or explains the various text structures found in informational texts. The internal text structure is made clear to students through the use of graphic organizers that match the hierarchical relationships among the ideas in a specific piece of text. The reader learns to recognize that the text patterns represent the different types of logical connections among the important and less important ideas in informational material.

Before Reading

First, the teacher analyzes the text by surveying it for important ideas and for transition words. Next, the instructor studies the content to locate what pattern connects the key ideas. Third, the teacher outlines or diagrams the relationships among the superordinate and coordinate ideas. Lastly, a graphic representation is made. The goal is for the teacher to explain to the students how these steps are done. The teacher goes through the process several times for each of the various types of internal text organizations (description, sequence, comparison-contrast, cause-effect, problem-solution, classification). As the students become familiar with a specific type of organization, the teacher gradually does less and less of the "before reading" process until the students are able to create their own graphical structure from analyzing the text by themselves. This step teaches the students to recognize a specific text structure.

During Reading

During reading, the students take notes on the specific text structure (description, sequence, comparison-contrast, cause-effect, problem-solution, classification) using a visual representation called an internal text structure frame.

After Reading

Students now write a summary of the information in the frame. Framed paragraphs that match the visual graphic representation of the hierarchical organization of the text are used to guide the students to the writing of a well-organized summary that matches the text structure and includes all the important information. Ideas that support the main idea are important information. Within the framed paragraphs, appropriate transition words and phrases are modeled.

Again, the goal of this process is first, guide the students through the steps, then gradually allow the students to have independent ownership of this strategy, which leads to meaningful learning. Recognizing logical connections through text structure accommodates student metacognition.

Internal Text Structure

Where can teachers find examples to model text structure? The following list of informational books represents the informational text structure available for teacher use.

P = primary grades (K–2)   M = middle grades (3–5)   U = upper grades (6–8)

Description

Balestrino, P. (1971). *The Skeleton Inside You*. New York: Crowell. (P)

Branley, F. M. (1986). *What the Moon Is Like*. New York: Harper & Row. (M)

Hansen, R., & Bell, R. A. (1985). *My First Book of Space*. New York: Simon & Schuster. (M)

Horvatic, A. (1989). *Simple Machines*. New York: Dutton. (M)

Parish, P. (1974). *Dinosaur Time*. New York: Harper & Row. (P)

Sequence

Carrick, C. (1978). *Octopus*. New York: Clarion. (M)

Cole, J. (1991). *My Puppy Is Born*. New York: Morrow. (P–M)

Gibbons, G. (1985). *Lights! Camera! Action!* New York: Crowell. (M)

Jaspersohn, W. (1988). *Ice Cream*. New York: Macmillan. (M–U)

Lasky, K. (1983). *Sugaring Time*. New York: Macmillan. (M–U)

Macaulay, D. (1977). *Castle*. Boston: Houghton Mifflin. (M–U)

Provensen, A. (1980). *The Buck Stops Here*. New York: Harper-Collins. (M–U)

Comparison

Gibbons, G. (1984). *Fire! Fire!* New York: Harper & Row. (P–M)

Lasker, J. (1976). *Merry Ever After: The Story of Two Medieval Weddings*. New York: Viking. (M–U)

Rowan, J. P. (1985). *Butterflies and Moths (A New True Book)*. Chicago: Children's Press. (M)

Spier, P. (1987). *We the People*. New York: Doubleday. (M–U)

Cause and Effect

Branley, F. M. (1985). *Flash, Crash, Rumble and Roll*. New York: Harper & Row. (P–M)

Branley, F. M. (1985). *Volcanoes*. New York: Harper & Row. (P–M)

Branley, F. M. (1986). *What Makes Day and Night?* New York: Harper & Row. (P–M)

Selsam, M. E. (1981). *Where Do They Go? Insects in Winter*. New York: Scholastic. (P–M)

Showers, P. (1985). *What Happens to a Hamburger?* New York: Harper & Row. (P–M)

Problem and Solution

Cole, J. (1983). *Cares and How They Go.* New York: Harper & Row. (P–M)

Horwitz, J. (1984). *Night Markets: Bringing Food to the City.* New York: Harper & Row. (M–U)

Lauber, P. (1990). *How We Learned the Earth Is Round.* New York: Crowell. (P–M)

Levine, E. (1988). *If You Traveled on the Underground Railroad.* New York: Scholastic. (P–M)

Showers, P. (1980). *No Measles, No Mumps for Me.* New York: Crowell. (P–M)

Simon, S. (1984). *The Dinosaur Is the Biggest Animal That Ever Lived and Other Wrong Ideas You Thought Were Right.* New York: Harper & Row. (P–M)

Combination

Aliki. (1981). *Digging Up Dinosaur*s. New York: Harper & Row. (M)

de Paola, T. (1978). *The Popcorn Book.* New York: Holiday House. (P–M)

Podenforf, I. (1982). *Jungles (A New True Book).* Chicago: Childrens Press. (M)

Sabin, S. (1985). *Amazing World of Ants.* Manwah, NJ: Troll. (M)

Venutra, P., & Ceserani, G. P. (1985). *In Search of Tutankhamun.* Morristown, NJ: Silver Burdett. (U)

Source: Tompkins, Gail E., *Teaching Writing: Balancing Process and Product,* 2nd edition, © 1994. Reprinted by permission of Pearson Education, Inc., Upper Saddle River, NJ.

Internal Text Structure

Problem and Solution Text

Who has the problem? _____

What is the problem? _____

_____

Why is it a problem? _____

Action Taken/Possible Solutions

Results

Key Questions

What is the problem?
Who had the problem?
Why was it a problem?
What attempts were made to solve the
    problem?
What was the end result?

Transition Words

Because	If . . . then,	therefore
Consequently	as a result	so that
This led to	nevertheless	since
accordingly	thus	

Summary Pattern:

_____ had a problem because _____.

Therefore, _____.

As a result, _____.

MODEL/TEMPLATE OF READING STRATEGY

Internal Text Structure

Sequential Text

General Frame: The author is putting facts, events, or concepts into an identifiable sequence.

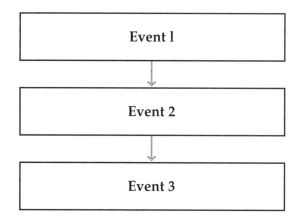

Key Questions

What is the object, procedure, or
   initiating event?
What are the stages or steps?
How do they lead to one another?
What is the final outcome?

Transition Words

first,	next	then
finally	last	before
later	soon	as
meanwhile	then	dates
ages	time of day	seasons

Summary Pattern:

Here is how _____ is

made/occurs. First, _____. Next,

_____. Then _____.

Finally, _____.

MODEL / TEMPLATE OF READING STRATEGY

Internal Text Structure

Cause and Effect Text

General Frame: The author is showing how concepts, facts, or events happen because of other concepts, facts, or events.

Cause	Cause

Effect

Key Questions

What were the causes?
What were the effects?
What was the initiating event?
What are the chain reactions of cause
  and effect?

Transition Words

because	since	so
as a result	consequently	therefore

Summary Pattern:

Because of _____, _____,

_____ causes _____.

Therefore _____. Finally, due to

_____, _____.

This explains why _____.

Internal Text Structure

Compare/Contrast Text

General Frame: The author is pointing out likenesses and differences in concepts, facts, or events.

List how _____ & _____ are alike.
1.
2.
3.
4.
5.

List how _____ & _____ are different.

Features or Attributes		
1.	1.	1.
2.	2.	2.
3.	3.	3.
4.	4.	4.
5.	5.	5.
6.	6.	6.
7.	7.	7.

(continued)

MODEL/TEMPLATE OF READING STRATEGY

Internal Text Structure

Compare/Contrast Text (*continued*)

Key Questions

What things are being compared?
How are they similar?
How are they different?

Transition Words

however	unlike	by contrast
in comparison	although	yet
similar to	but	different from
while	in addition	finally

Summary Pattern:

Comparison

_____ and _____ are similar in several

ways. Both _____ and _____,

_____ . _____ and

_____ have similar _____.

Finally, both _____ and _____ _____.

Contrast

_____ and _____ are different in several ways.

First of all, _____, while _____. Secondly,

_____ but _____. In addition,

while _____, _____. Finally,

_____ _____, while _____.

MODEL/TEMPLATE OF READING STRATEGY

Internal Text Structure

Description Text

General Frame: The author is connecting ideas through listing important characteristics or attributes of the topic.

Topic

Attribute

Attribute

Attribute

Key Questions

What is the topic? What is most important? What are other factors?

Transition Words

to begin with   also most important   in fact for example

Summary Pattern:

To begin with, _____.

Most important _____, also,

_____. In fact, _____.

For example, _____.

Internal Text Structure

Classification Text

_____

Title of chapter or subsection

Subheading	Subheading	Subheading
(Supporting details)	(Supporting details)	(Supporting details)

Key Questions

What is the superordinate category?
What are the subordinate categories?
How are they related?
How many levels are there?

Transition Words

such as	for example
specifically	in particular
in addition	it is related

Summary Paragraph:

_____ is the title of the selection. Three categories or classifications

are part of this topic. The first classification is _____.

Some examples are _____.

The second classification is _____.

In particular, _____.

The third classification is _____.

Specifically, _____.

These categories are related _____.

CHAPTER EIGHT

Integration of Strategies

Integration of Strategies

Social Science
Anticipation Guide
Two-Column Notes
Four-Step Summary

Language Arts
Prediction Pairs
Internal Text Structure
Incomplete Paragraph
    Frame

Math
KWLH+
Internal Text Structure
Incomplete Paragraph
    Frame

Science
Partner Knowledge
    Rater+
Stop-the-Process
GIST

Physical Education
Partner Knowledge
    Rater+
Heading through a
    Picture Walk
Incomplete Paragraph
    Frame

Fine Arts
Think-Aloud with
    Questions
Reader Response
    Journal
Incomplete Paragraph
    Frame

Foreign Language
Picture Walk
List-Group-Label
GRASP the Heading

Many strategies have been introduced in this book. Now that these strategies have been presented and practiced, it is time to see how they can be integrated in creative ways to benefit student comprehension and vocabulary development. Greater understanding can be achieved through the integration of more than one strategy with a piece of complex text. This chapter will highlight pieces of text and show how to integrate several strategies within a lesson. Remember, differing strategies can be integrated before reading the material, during the reading of the material, and after reading the material.

By differentiating instruction, the learning styles of all students will be met. Students will begin to determine which strategy they need to use to help them learn. The goal of teaching strategies is to have the strategies become student owned.

The following table and chapter will give teachers an example of the before, during, and after strategies to use on various content area subject matter.

Integration of Strategies

Subject	Before Reading	During Reading	After Reading
Social Studies	**Anticipation Guide** *Chapter Two* Prior Knowledge	**Two-Column Notes** *Chapter Three* Instructional Frames	**Four-Step Summary** *Chapter Six* Writing to Learn
Language Arts	**Prediction Pairs** *Chapter Three* Instructional Frames	**Internal Text Structure** (Problem/Solution) *Chapter Seven* Studying Text	**Incomplete Paragraph Frame** (Problem/Solution) *Chapter Six* Writing to Learn
Math	**KWLH+** *Chapter Two* Prior Knowledge	**Internal Text Structure** (Sequence) *Chapter Seven* Studying Text	**Incomplete Paragraph Frame** (Sequence) *Chapter Six* Writing to Learn
Science	**Knowledge Rater+** *Chapter Four* Vocabulary	**Stop-the-Process** *Chapter Five* Talking to Learn	**GIST** *Chapter Six* Writing to Learn
Physical Education	**Partner Knowledge Rater+** *Chapter Four*	**Heading through a Picture Walk** *Chapter Two* Prior Knowledge	**Framed Paragraph** (Classification) *Chapter Five* Writing to Learn
Fine Arts Music Art Dance and Drama	**Think-Aloud with Questions** *Chapter Two* Prior Knowledge	**Reader-Response Journal** (Visualization Format) *Chapter Five* Writing to Learn	**Incomplete Paragraph Frame** (Sequence) *Chapter Five* Writing to Learn
Foreign Language	**Picture Walk** *Chapter Two* Prior Knowledge **List-Group-Label** *Chapter Four* Vocabulary	**GRASP the Headings** *Chapter Six* Writing to Learn	**GRASP the Headings** *Chapter Six* Writing to Learn

Model of Reading Strategy

Before Reading **Anticipation Guide**

Directions: Put a check under "likely" if you feel that the statement is true. Put a check under "unlikely" if you feel that it has no truth. Be ready to explain your choices.

Before Reading			*After Reading*	
Likely	**Unlikely**		**Likely**	**Unlikely**
_____	_____	1. Popular sovereignty is guaranteed in the Constitution and means that some people are more popular than others.	_____	_____
_____	_____	2. The system of three branches of government (Legislative, Judicial, and Executive) provides for checks and balances on each branch.	_____	_____
_____	_____	3. Federalism divides power between the national government and the state government.	_____	_____
_____	_____	4. Because of the Bill of Rights, all Americans can do what they want.	_____	_____

After reading correct your anticipation guide.

Model of Reading Strategy

During Reading   **Two-Column Notes**

The Principles of the Constitution	
Headings and Key Terms	*Reading Notes*
The People Rule	*"We the People"*
Popular sovereignty	*People hold final authority in government*
Representative Government	*The People elect public officials to make laws and other decisions for them*
Limited Government	*The government only has the power that the people specifically grant to it.*
Guarantees of Liberty	*The limits on government are in the Bill of Rights, which guarantees individual liberty.*
Federalism	*Two governments: national government concerns itself with national concerns; state governments meet local needs. Listed powers for central government*
Powers of the States	*All the rest of the powers belong to the states. All states represented in federal government. All states equal in manner of trade*
The "Law of the Land"	*Is the Federal Constitution*
Separation of Powers	*Power of federal government divided between three branches*
Legislative Branch	*Makes the laws*
Executive Branch	*Carries out the laws*
Judicial Branch	*Interprets the laws*
Checks and Balances	*Each branch checks or controls the power of the two branches*

Checks on Congress
   Bills
   Voting
   Unconstitutional
	
	Proposed laws-Legislative
	Rejecting a bill-Executive
	Not permitted by the Constitution-Judicial

Checks on the President Overriding	*Senate must ratify treaties that the President makes* *Congress can set aside a presidential veto*
Checks on the Courts	*President and Congress check on the power of the Judicial branch* *President appoints federal judges; senate approves the President's court appointments* *Congress can remove federal judges if found guilty of wrongdoing* *Congress may propose a constitutional amendment to overrule judge's decision*

WRITING TO LEARN

Model of Reading Strategy

After Reading   ## Four-Step Summary

What are you summarizing?	What does it begin with?	What is in the middle?	How does it end?
There are five principles to the Constitution: 1. People Rule 2. Limited Government 3. Federalism 4. Separation of Powers 5. Checks and Balances	1. People Rule—popular sovereignty means people have final authority over government. 2. Limited government—only the power that the people give it. People elect public officials to make laws and other decisions for them. The limits on government are in the Bill of Rights, which guarantees individual liberty.	3. Two governments: National government concerns itself with national issues; state governments meet local needs. There are listed powers for the central government. All the rest of the powers belong to the states. All states are represented in federal government. All states equal in matters of trade. The law of the land is the federal Constitution. 4. Separation of powers means the federal government divides its power between the three branches: legislative, executive, and judicial. Legislative—makes law Executive—enforces law Judicial—interprets law	5. The checks and balances mean that each branch checks or controls the power of the other two branches. The legislative branch proposes laws, the executive vetoes or rejects a bill from the legislature, and the judicial branch finds laws unconstitutional or not permitted by the Constitution. The executive branch is checked by the Senate having to ratify treaties made by the President, and Congress can set aside a Presidential veto. Checks on the court are that the President appoints federal judges and the Senate approves the President's court appointments. Congress can remove federal judges if found guilty of wrongdoing. Congress may propose a constitutional amendment to overrule judge's decisions.

The five basic principles in the United States Constitution are (1) Popular Sovereignty, people have the final authority over government; (2) Limited Government, people elect public officials to make laws and the public power is limited by the Bill of Rights; (3) Federalism, the national government concerns itself with national issues while state governments meet local needs; (4) Separation of powers refers to the division of power between the three branches; (5) Checks and Balances were created in order for each branch to retain power over the other two branches. The United States Constitution is the law of the land and distributes power and authority between the three branches: legislative, executive, and judicial as well as federal and state powers.

Model of Reading Strategy

Before Reading   **Prediction Pairs**

"Raymond's Run" by Toni Cade Bambara

As the teacher reads the first two paragraphs of the story aloud, the students listen for the characters, setting, and problem. The following is a short summary of the first two paragraphs of "Raymond's Run" from *Gorilla, My Love* by Toni Cade Bambara. Be prepared to predict what will happen next.

Squeaky introduces hereslf to the reader by relating that one of her main jobs is taking care of her bigger, older brother, Raymond, who is mentally challenged. People say mean things to Raymond because of his enlarged head, but Squeaky will not stand for any nonsense. She readily answers "put downs" from the "bad mouthing" neighborhood crowd by willingly fighting anyone who insults her brother.

Squeaky (nickname Mercury) is the fastest runner in New York City's Harlem district. She wins the May Day Race every year. This year she is challenged by Gretchen who is spreading rumors that she is going to beat Squeaky in the race. In addition, the race coordinator indicates to Squeaky that perhaps it is time for someone else to win. Squeaky is disconcerted with the rumors and with the idea that she has to constantly practice to be number one while others like Gretchen breeze through situations without hard work.

Prediction Pair   _Susan_   _Michel_

From what you have learned, make a prediction and tell why you think so.

The first person in the pair: What is going to happen next? *The girl is going to win the race.*	**First person in the pair:** What makes you think so? *Squeaky said she is the fastest runner next to her father.*
Second person in the pair: What is going to happen next? *Someone tries to beat up on her brother.*	**Second person in the pair:** What makes you think so? *Squeaky said that if someone bothers her brother, she'd rather knock him or her down than talk.*

Information Source: "Raymond's Run," copyright © 1971 by Toni Cade Bambara, from *Gorilla, My Love* by Toni Cade Bambara.

Model of Reading Strategy

During Reading

Internal Text Structure

Problem/Solution Text

Who has the Problem? *Squeaky (nickname Mercury) has a problem.*

What is the Problem? *She takes care of her mentally challenged brother, Raymond, and she practices her running form, speed, and endurance whenever and wherever she can.*

Why is it a Problem?
- *Squeaky is frustrated by a girl in her class, Cynthia, who always does well on tests, spelling bees, and piano recitals, yet acts like she never practices.*
- *Squeaky is confronted by a girl named Gretchen, who makes fun of Raymond and says that she is going to beat Squeaky in the May race.*
- *The race coordinator, Mr. Pearson, suggests that Squeaky allow someone else to win this year's race because she wins all the time.*

Action Taken/Possible Solutions

1. *Practices her running all the time.*
2. *She fights anyone who makes fun of Raymond.*
3. *Squeaky uses "put-downs" on girls who smart-talk her.*
4. *Squeaky looks at Mr. Pearson as if he is out of his mind.*

Results

1. *Squeaky wins the May Day Race.*
2. *Other people are more careful and do not make fun of Raymond.*
3. *The girls do not have a comeback. Gretchen comes in a close second in the May Day Race.*
4. *Squeaky sees Raymond running the race with her outside the fence and realizes that he has talent as a runner.*
5. *If someone beats Squeaky someday, she realizes that she can do many things, including coaching Raymond.*

Model of Reading Strategy

After Reading **Incomplete Paragraph Frame**

Problem and Solution Summary Frame

State who has a problem and what the problem is.

Squeaky is responsible for her mentally challenged brother, Raymond; consequently, her classmates and others make fun of her brother. Squeaky is frustrated by classmates who exhibit their talents and claim they never have to practice while she continually practices her running. Gretchen claims she will beat Squeaky in the May Day Race while the race coordinator tells her it is time to let someone else win the race.

Tell what action was taken to try to solve the problem.

As a solution to the above-mentioned problems, Squeaky constantly practices her running, she fights people who make fun of her brother, and she answers back or just ignores anyone who tries to intimidate her.

Tell what happened as a result of the action taken.

As a result, when Gretchen does come in a very close second in the race, Squeaky learns to respect her and realizes that the day may come when she will not win the race. During the race, Squeaky notices that Raymond, who is running on the other side of the fence, runs the race with her. As a result, Squeaky realizes that when she no longer wins first place in races, she can do many things, including coaching her brother.

Summary:

Squeaky had a problem because she is responsible for her mentally challenged brother, Raymond; consequently, her classmates and others make fun of her brother. Squeaky is frustrated by classmates who exhibit their talents and claim they never have to practice while she continually practices her running. Gretchen claims she will beat Squeaky in the May Day Race while the race coordinator tells her it is time to let someone else win the race. As a solution to the above-mentioned problems, Squeaky constantly practices her running, she fights people who make fun of her brother, and she answers back or just ignores anyone who tries to intimidate her. As a result, when Gretchen does come in a very close second in the race, Squeaky learns to respect her and realizes that the day may come when she will not win the race. During the race, Squeaky notices that Raymond, who is running on the other side of the fence, runs the race with her. As a result, Squeaky realizes that when she no longer wins first place in races, she can do many things, including coaching her brother.

KWLH+

Directions: Brainstorm what is already known about this type of problem. As questions arise, place them under the want to know column.

The problem: Find the sum. Simplify. $\frac{2}{3} + \frac{3}{4}$		
K **Known**	**W** **Want to know**	**L** **Learned**
Find a common denominator.	What number is the lowest common denominator?	12
Rename both fractions as equivalent fractions. Add the numerators.	How is this done again with multiplying the numbers in a criss-cross fashion?	$\bullet \quad \frac{2}{3} + \frac{3}{4}$ $\frac{8}{12} + \frac{9}{12} =$
Reduce the answer to a mixed number.	$\frac{17}{12} =$ Do I divide numerator by denominator?	Yes. 1 5/12

Model of Reading Strategy

Internal Text Structure

Sequence with Process Notes for Math

THINK—What is the question: What are you being asked to do? Rewrite the question.
The problem: Find the sum. Simplify. $\frac{2}{3} + \frac{3}{4}$

SOLVE—What is your mathematical plan? Show your work.

Step 1	Step 2	Step 3
$\frac{2}{3} + \frac{3}{4} =$	$\frac{8}{12} + \frac{9}{12} =$	$\frac{8}{12} + \frac{9}{12} = \frac{17}{12} = 1\ 5/12$

EXPLAIN—What was your thought process? How did you solve the problem?

First I . . .	Then I . . .	And finally I . . .
1. I have to find a common denominator. 2. Divide the present denominators into the common denominator. 3. Multiply the numerators by what was divided into the denominator. 4. Add the numerators. 5. Make a mixed number.	found my common denominator. How many times does 3 go into 12? (4) (4) times (2) is 8. 2 now becomes <u>8</u>. How many times does 4 go into 12? (3) (3) times (3) is 9. 3 now becomes <u>9</u>.	Add 8 + 9, which equals 17 over the denominator $\frac{17}{12}$ Which is reduced to 1 and 5/12.

After Reading   **Incomplete Paragraph Frame**

Sequence

State the main idea.

Find the sum and simplify the answer. $\frac{2}{3} + \frac{3}{4} =$

First

I have to find a common denominator.

Then

Once I have found my common denominator, I have to rename the fractions as equivalents. Add the numerators.

Finally

Simplify, or reduce the answer to its lowest terms.

Summary:

First, I have to find a common denominator. Then, once I have found my common denominator, I have to rename the fractions as equivalents. Add the numerators. Finally, simplify, or reduce the answer to its lowest terms.

Model of Reading Strategy

Before Reading **Partner Knowledge Rater+**

Define the following words	On my own, first try (guess or draw)	With a partner, second try (discuss, agree)	After reading, or glossary definition
Charge			
Static electricity			
Electric current			
Circuit			
Electric cell			
Conductor			
Insulator			
Resistor			
Electric field			
Positive charge			
Negative charge			
Parallel circuit			
Series circuit			

During Reading   **Stop-the-Process**

Electricity

Chapter ___ / Science   **Fourth Grade**

_____   _____
Name   Date

---

1. Read pages ___ - ___
Two Kinds of Charge
Charge is _____
_____
Static electricity is _____
What are the two types of charges?

Separating Charges
An object with a _____ charge
has more negative particles than positive.

Only _____ charges move.

---

2. Read pages ___ - ___ **Electric Forces**

An electric field is _____
_____.

The balloons with opposite charges
_____ each other.

When two objects both have positive
charges the objects _____.

---

3. Read pages ___ - ___ **Moving Charges**
Electric current is _____
A circuit is _____
An electric cell is _____

Controlling Current
A conductor will _____

A good conductor material is _____.
The job of the insulator is
_____.

A good insulator is _____.
A resistor _____
_____.

The metal coil in a bulb is a resistor. As
charges move through this coil, the charges
heat up and glow, giving off light.

---

4. Read pages ___ - ___. **Series and
Parallel Circuits**

Draw a **series circuit.**
Explain how it works.

Draw a **parallel circuit.**
Explain how it works.

GIST

Directions: Create a summary relating to the two concepts listed below using only *twenty words.* Work in pairs to complete the GIST, and then share your GIST with another pair. Revisions and collaborations may be shared, and then presented to the teacher and entire class. The class will agree on a main idea summary for each concept.

What Is Static Electricity?

Gaining or losing negative charges causes electric charge or electric field. Charged objects interact. Like charges repel, unlike charges attract.

What Is Electric Current?

Electric current consists of flowing charges through a circuit. A single path for current is called series, more paths, and parallel.

Model of Reading Strategy

Before Reading   **Partner Knowledge Rater+**

Directions: In column one, the students draw a picture or put down words that help them understand the vocabulary words for General Rules, Defense, and Offense. After a few minutes, the students share their responses with partners and add new learnings in the second column. We will return for column three at the conclusion of the lesson.

General Rules

Define the Following Words	First try by yourself	Second try with partner	Third after reading
Mental endurance			
Physical endurance			
Center			
Free throw line			
Guards			
Jump ball			
Dribble			
Field goal			
Three point line			
Personal foul			
Technical foul			

(continued)

PRIOR KNOWLEDGE

Model of Reading Strategy

Before Reading **Partner Knowledge Rater+** *(continued)*

Defense

Define the Following Words	First try by yourself	Second try with partner	Third after reading
Zone defense			
Player to player defense			

Offense

Define the Following Words	First try by yourself	Second try with partner	Third after reading
Fast break style			
Slow break style			

INSTRUCTIONAL FRAMES

Model of Reading Strategy

During Reading   **Heading through a Picture Walk**

Directions: After examining the pictures and previewing headings, the students put the vocabulary words under the appropriate headings. As they read, they place drawn pictures or written notes under the correct heading.

How the Game Is Played

General Playing Rules

Mental & physical endurance
Need Skills
Team: two forwards, two guards, & center
Start with jump ball
Dribble ball down the floor
Pass by throwing ball
A field goal is a 2-point basket
Three point is 20'-6" away from basket.
Free throw if fouled
Personal foul—push or trip
Technical foul—game delay or shows disrespect
Traveling—run or walk with ball

Defense

Zone—each player as a guard in the zone under the basket

Player-player, man-to-man

Offense

Fast break— quick passes & more players on the attack

Slow break— players maneuver to shoot

WRITING TO LEARN

Model of Reading Strategy

After Reading   **Incomplete Paragraph Frame**

Classification

Directions: Using the headings and the notes under the headings, the students write a summary of the article on basketball. Finally, return to prereading vocabulary to confirm word meaning.

The game of basketball takes mental and physical endurance along with many skills. The team is composed of two forwards, two guards, and a center. The game starts with a jump ball. The players then dribble the ball down the court, or they pass by throwing the ball. A field goal occurs when a player puts the ball through the basket. A three-point field goal occurs when the ball is thrown from beyond 20 feet 6 inches. A player gets a free throw if he is fouled. A personal foul involves pushing or tripping while a technical foul involves a delay of game or a show of disrespect. Traveling is called if a player runs or walks with the ball.

The first type of defense is zone defense. Each player acts as a guard in the area under the basket. The second type of defense is player to player. In this case, each player guards a specific person.

The fast break is a type of offense. This means the players make quick passes and more players are on the attack. The slow break means the players maneuver in order to get a good shot at the basket.

Model of Reading Strategy

Think-Aloud with Questions
Nutcracker Suite:
Music by Peter Tchaikovsky

1. The teacher presents a short summary or video of the life of Tchaikovsky.

2. The names of the four sections of the music and ballet are put on the board: Christmas Eve, Battle with the Mice, the Land of Sweets, and the Sugar Plum Fairy.

3. The key elements of the first section are shown and explained to the students: Musical Note, the Children on Stage, Herr Drosselmeyer, the Nutcracker, and the Grandfather Dance.

4. A Think-Aloud with Questions on the first section, Christmas Eve, is modeled with the students.

Think-Aloud with Questions
The teacher gives the students a copy of text containing the beginning of the selection that has been prepared with a space of about one inch between sentences. The class and the teacher do a Picture Walk through the first section of the musical story. The teacher starts reading the passage, stopping after every sentence or two. The students then write their predictions on their paper, underneath the appropriate sentence. The students then share their predictions, images, and analogies with each other and then the class.

Christmas Eve. Text: One frosty Christmas Eve many years ago, a family by the name of Stahlbaum gave a big, festive party. When the guests arrived, everyone went to the drawing room to see the Christmas tree and all the presents.

• How do you feel before a holiday when presents are exchanged?

Clara's godfather arrives with his nephew. Herr Drosselmeyer, the godfather, takes a painted wooden soldier out of his pocket and shows Clara how to crack nuts between its hinged jaws. Drosselmeyer's nephew, Fritz, grabs for it and it falls and breaks on the floor.

• How would you feel if a present you are about to receive is broken by a relative?

Drosselmeyer bandages the nutcracker's head, and Clara kisses her nutcracker and puts it into her doll's bed.

• What do you think will happen to the nutcracker during the night?

Questions:

Who is the main character?

What are the names of the other important characters?

What is the setting?

What is going to happen during the night when everyone is sleeping?

The before-reading Picture Walk and questioning process is repeated for the other three sections of the ballet: the Battle with the Mice, the Land of Sweets, and the Sugar Plum Fairy.

Model of Reading Strategy

During Reading

Response Journal

Visualization

1. The students read the first section, Christmas Eve.

2. They listen to the music of the Christmas Eve section.

3. After reading the story and listening to the music, they draw the part or parts they were able to visualize from reading the story and listening to the music.

4. Under the picture or on the back of the picture, each student writes what his or her individual picture illustrates from the Christmas Eve section of the musical ballet.

On Christmas Eve, Clara and her family have a big party. Clara is given a nutcracker by her godfather, Herr Drosselmeyer. His nephew, Fritz, grabs the nutcracker and it breaks. Drosselmeyer repairs it, and Clara puts it into her doll's bed.

This same process is repeated for the following three sections:

Battle with the Mice

The Land of Sweets

The Sugar Plum Fairy

1. The students read the previewed section.

2. They listen to the music for that section.

3. Then they draw a picture of the part or parts they were best able to visualize.

4. Lastly, they write a sentence describing what they drew.

Model of Reading Strategy

After Reading   ## Incomplete Paragraph Frame

Sequence

The students write a summary of the Nutcracker Suite by combining the sentences they wrote on each of the four pictures they visualized from reading the story and listening to the music.

Christmas Eve

On Christmas Eve, Clara and her family have a big party. Clara is given a nutcracker by her godfather, Herr Drosselmeyer. His nephew, Fritz, grabs the nutcracker and it breaks. Drosselmeyer repairs it, and Clara puts it into her doll's bed.

Battle with the Mice

Clara goes down to the drawing room in the middle of the night to check on the nutcracker. She meets an army of mice. Fritz's tin soldiers and the nutcracker fight the mice. Clara helps by throwing her slipper at the Mouse King. The nutcracker kills the Mouse King and the mice run away. Fritz appears as a prince and leads Clara into the snow.

The Land of Sweets

They enter the kingdom and palace of the Sugar Plum Fairy. Clara and Fritz sit on the Sugar Plum Fairy's throne and watch the Chocolate do the Spanish dance followed by Arabian Coffee, Chinese Tea, Russian peppermints, and lastly, a flock of marzipan shepherdesses.

The Sugar Plum Fairy

Mother Ginger enters the throne room, and her children play around her. Next the candied flowers dance. Finally the Sugar Plum Fairy dances and is joined by her prince. At the end, Clara kisses and thanks the Sugar Plum Fairy. Fritz and Clara set off to explore their future.

Sources:

The Illustrated Book of Ballet Stories, written by Barbara Newman and illustrated by Gill Tomblin. New York: DK Publishing Book, 1997, 53–61.

Lives of the Musicians: Good Times, Bad Times, and What the Neighbors Thought, by Kathleen Krull. San Diego: Harcourt Brace Jovanovich, 1993, 55–57.

Model of Reading Strategy

Before Reading

Picture Walk
List-Group-Label

Spanish One
En Colores: Culturas Y Comparaciones
"Beisbol: El Pasatiempo Nacional"

Directions: The teacher guides the students through a picture walk through the section.

1. The students individually scan the four paragraphs of text on baseball in Puerto Rico and Latin America and write down words they know.

2. Students share the words they know with a partner along with telling their partner what they think the article is going to say about baseball in Puerto Rico.

3. The teacher introduces the Spanish vocabulary words that are present in the article.

Sports Words and Phrases

team	el equipo
to win	ganar conjugated
to play	jugar(ue) conjugated
game	el partido
sporting goods store	la tienda de deportes

Equipment			Location		
bat	el bate		outdoors	al aire libre	
ball	la bola		field	el campo	
helmet	el casco				
baseball cap	la gorra				
glove	el guante				
baseball	la pelota				

4. The students make a card for each word. On the front of the card is the Spanish word with a picture, and on the back is the English word and a Spanish sentence that uses the target word. The cards are sorted into piles and labeled *Sport Words and Phrases, Equipment,* and *Location.*

WRITING TO LEARN

Model of Reading Strategy

During Reading   ## GRASP the Headings

Directions:

1. The teacher lists the main ideas in the form of headings on the board.
2. The students listen to the teacher or a tape of the baseball article.
3. The students read the three-paragraph article by themselves.
4. The students record in Spanish under the correct heading the information they learn from the article.
5. This information is shared in Spanish with a partner and then the class.
6. The students read the article a second time adding more information under each heading. This is again shared with a partner and then with the class. The following example is done in Spanish.

Puerto Rico

Baseball is popular
October to March
Played in major cities in Puerto Rico
U.S. major and minor leagues play in Puerto Rico.

The Coliseo Roberto Clemente

Played for the Pittsburgh Pirates
Major League Puerto Rican Player
In the Hall of Fame
The baseball coliseum is named for Roberto Clemente.

Other Caribbean Nations and Their Baseball Heroes

Juan Marichal of Dominican Republic, in Hall of Fame
Andres Galarraga of Venezuela
Edgar Renteria of Columbia
Livan Hernandez of Cuba
Fernando Valenzuela of Mexico
All are important baseball players in the Major Leagues in the U.S.

WRITING TO LEARN

Model of Reading Strategy

GRASP the Headings

Directions: The students write a summary in Spanish by combining each heading and its informational notes into one or two Spanish sentences. Thus, the summary paragraph will have three to six Spanish sentences. The following is an example:

Baseball is very popular in Puerto Rico. This country supplies players to the major and minor baseball leagues in the United States. Roberto Clemente is from Puerto Rico and he played for the Pittsburgh Pirates. He not only is in the Baseball Hall of Fame, but he also has a coliseum in Puerto Rico named after him. Other Latin American nations have famous United States of America baseball players: Juan Marichal of the Dominican Republic, Andrew Galarraga of Venezuela, Edgar Renteria of Columbia, Livan Hernandez of Cuba, and Fernando Valenzuela of Mexico.

The students share their written paragraphs with each other and the class. The students continue to review the categorized baseball vocabulary words. As they read and learn more about baseball in Latin America, they will add to their summary of the unit.

Source: En Espanol, 1 Uno. (2004). Evanston, IL: McDougal Littell, A Houghton Mifflin Company, pages 212–217.

Bibliography

Afflerbach, P. P. (1986). The influence of prior knowledge on expert readers' importance assignment processes. In J. A. Niles & R. V. Lalik (Eds.), *Solving problems in literacy: Learners, teachers and researchers* (pp. 30–40). Rochester, NY: National Reading Conference.

Allen, J. (2000). *Yellow brick roads: Shared and guided paths to independent reading.* Portland, ME: Stenhouse.

Allington, R. (1994). *Research based programs.* New York: Longman.

Alvermann, D. (1991). The discussion web: A graphic aid for learning across the curriculum. *The Reading Teacher, 45,* 92–99.

Anderson, R. C., & Pearson, D. D. (1984). Schema-theoretic view of basic process in reading comprehension. In D. Pearson et al. (Eds.), *Handbook of Reading Research,* 255–291. New York: Longman.

Anderson, R. C., Reynolds, R. E., Schallert, D. C., & Goetz, E. T. (1977). Frameworks for comprehension discourse. *American Education Research Journal, 14.*

Anderson, R. C., Wilson, P., & Fielding, L. (1988). Growth in reading and how children spend their time outside of school. *Reading Research Quarterly, 23,* 285–303.

Andre, J. D., & Anderson, T. H. (1979). The development and evaluation of a self-questioning study technique. *Reading Research Quarterly, 14.*

Andrews, S. E. (October, 1997). Writing to learn in content area reading class. *Journal of Adolescent & Adult Literacy, 41,* 2, 141–142.

Armbruster, B. B., & Anderson, T. H. (1984). *Producing considerate expository text.* Champaign: University of Illinois, Center for the Study of Reading.

Armbruster, B., Anderson, T., & Stertag, J. (1989). Teaching text structure to improve reading and writing. *The Reading Teacher,* 130–137. Newark, DE: International Reading Association.

Armbruster, B., & Osborn, J. (2001). *Put reading first: The research building blocks for teaching children to read.* Washington, DC: The U.S. Department of Education.

Aronson, E. (1978). *The jigsaw classroom.* Thousand Oaks, CA: Sage.

Artley, A. S. (1975). Words, words, words. *Language Arts, 52,* 1067–1072.

Atwell, N. (1990). Introduction. In N. Atwell (Ed.), *Coming to know: Writing to learn in the intermediate grades* (pp. xii–xxiii). Portsmouth, NH: Heinemann.

Bambara, T. C. (1971). Raymond's run. In T. C. Bambara, *Gorilla, my love.* New York: Random House.

Barnes, D., Britton, J., & Rosen, H. (1969). *Language, the learner, and school.* New York: Penguin.

Bartlett, B. J. (1978). *Top-level structure as an organizational strategy for recall of classroom text.* Doctoral Dissertation. Arizonia State University.

Bechtel, J. (1985). *Improving writing and learning: A handbook for teachers in every class.* Boston: Allyn & Bacon.

Beck, I., & McKowen, M. (Nov.–Dec. 1981). Developing questions that promote comprehension: The story map. *Language Arts,* 913–918.

Beck, I. L., Perfetti, C. A., & McKeown, M. G. (1982). Effects of long-term vocabulary instruction on lexical access and reading comprehension. *Journal of Educational Psychology, 74.*

Berkowitz, S. J. (1986). Effects of instruction in text organization on sixth-grade students' memory for expository reading. *Reading Research Quarterly, 21,* 161–178.

Biemiller, A., & Meichenbaum, D. (1992). The nature and nurture of the self-directed learner. *Educational Leadership, 50*(2), 75–80.

Billings, H., & Billings, M. (1999). Climbing frozen waterfalls. *The Critical Reading Series, Daredevils.* Chicago, IL: Jamestown Publishers.

Billings, H., Billings, M., & Dramer, D. (1999). Black death: The end of the world. *The Critical Reading Series, Daredevils.* Chicago, IL: Jamestown Publishers.

Blachowicz. C. (1986). Making connections: Alternatives to the vocabulary notebook. *Journal of Reading, 29,* 643–649.

Blachowicz, C., & Fisher, P. (2002). *Teaching vocabulary in all classrooms.* Upper Saddle River, NJ: Merrill/Prentice Hall.

Blachowicz, C., & Ogle, D. (2001). *Reading comprehension: Strategies for independent learners.* New York: The Guilford Press.

Block, C. C., & Pressley, M. (Eds.). (2001). *Comprehension instruction: Research-based best practices.* New York: Guilford.

Bloomer, R. H. (1962). The cloze procedure as a remedial reading exercise. *Journal of Developmental Reading, 5,* 173–181.

Bluemfield, J. P., & Miller, G. R. (1966). Improving reading through teaching grammatical constraints. *Elementary English, 43,* 752–755.

Bower, B. H. (1970). Organizational factors in meaning. *Cognitive Psychology, 1.*

Bransford, J. D., & Johnson, M. K. (1972). Contextual

prerequisites for understanding: Some investigations of comprehension and recall. *Journal of Verbal Learning and Verbal Behavior, 11,* 717–726.

Britton, J., Burgess, T., Martin, T., McLeod, A., & Rosen, H. (1975). *The development of writing abilities.* London and Basingstoke, England: McMillan Ltd.

Brown, A. L., Campione, J. C., & Day, J. (1981). Learning to learn: On training students to learn from texts. *Educational Researcher, 10.*

Brown, A. L., & Smiley, S. S. (1977). Rating the importance of structural units of prose passages: A problem of metacognitive development. *Child Development, 48.*

Brozo, W. G. (1989). Applying a reader response heuristic to expository text. *Journal of Reading, 32,* 143–145.

Bruner, J. (1990). *Acts of meaning.* Cambridge, MA: Harvard University Press.

Bruner, J. S. (1982). *Child's talk.* London: Oxford University Press.

Buehl, D. (2003). *Classroom strategies for interactive learning.* Newark, DE: International Reading Association.

Carey, S. (1978). The child as word learner. In M. Halle, J. Bresnan, & G. A. Miller (Eds.), *Linguistic theory of psychological reality.* Cambridge, MA: The MIT Press.

Carr, E., & Ogle, D. (April, 1987). KWL plus: A strategy for comprehension and summarization. *Journal of Reading,* 626–631.

Carson, R. (2000). *Silent spring.* New York: Penguin Books.

Cawelti, G. (Ed.). (1999). *On improving student achievement.* Arlington, VA: Educational Research Service.

Clarke, M. (1991). *Discovering a respect: A handbook for student-directed group learning.* Seattle, WA: Goodwill Literacy Adult Learning Center, 1991. (ERIC Document Reproduction Service No. ED 355 346).

Cohen, R. (1983). Self-generated questions as an aid to reading comprehension. The Reading Teacher, 36.

"Cold Facts" (1998). *The Contemporary Reader, 2,* #5. Chicago, IL: Jamestown Publishers.

Cook, D. M. (1989). *Strategic learning in the content areas.* Madison, WI: Wisconsin Department of Public Instruction.

Craik, F. I., & Lockhart, R. S. (1972). Levels of processing: A framework for memory research. *Journal of Verbal Learning and Verbal Behavior, 11.*

Cunningham, J. W. (1982). Generating interactions between schemata and text. In J. A. Niles & L. A. Harris (Eds.), *New inquiries in reading research and instruction* (pp. 42–47). Rochester, NY: National Reading Conference.

Dale, E. (1965). Vocabulary measurement: Techniques and major findings. *Elementary English, 42,* 82–88.

Dansereau, D. F. (1987). Transfer from cooperative to individual studying. *Journal of Reading, 30.*

Davey, B. (October, 1983). Think aloud: Modeling the cognitive processes of reading comprehension. *Journal of Reading,* 44–47.

Davidson, J. L., & Wilkerson, B. C. (1988). *Directed reading-thinking activities.* Monroe, NY: Trillium Press.

Davis, F. B. (1968). Research in comprehension in reading. *Reading Research Quarterly, 3,* 499–545.

Dillon, J. T. (1981). Duration of response to teacher questions and statements. *Contemporary Educational Psychology, 6,* 1–11.

Doctorow, M., Wittrock, M. C., & Marks, C. (1978). Generative processes in reading comprehension. *Journal of Educational Psychology, 70.*

En Espanol. (2004). Evanston, IL: McDougal Littell.

Falk-Ross, F. C. (2002). *Classroom-based language and literacy intervention: A programs and case studies approach.* Boston, MA: Allyn & Bacon.

Falk-Ross, F. C. (1997). Developing metacommunicative awareness in children with language difficulties: Challenging the typical pull out system. *Language Arts, 74, 3,* 206–216.

Fass, W., & Schumacker, G. M. (1981). Schema theory and prose retention: Boundary conditions for encoding and retrieval effects. *Discourse Processes, 4.*

Frank, C. B. (1996). *Reading in the content areas: First, the questions.* Graduate class presentation for National Louis University at Lyons Township High School, LaGrange, IL.

Frank, C. B. (1998). *Improving vocabulary across the curriculum: Partner knowledge rater +.* Presentation at Shepard High School at Palos Heights, IL.

Frank, C. B. (1999). *Becoming an independent reader: KWLH+ and Concept Diagram.* Graduate presentation at Aurora University in Western Springs, IL.

Frank, C. B. (2000). *Critical thinking summary and RIVET: Improving vocabulary across the curriculum.* Presentation at Shepard High School in Palos Heights, IL.

Frank, C. B. (2001). *Reading, writing, learning strategies for the ESL student: Stop the process and think aloud with questions.* Workshop presentation to Denver Public School ESL teachers in Denver, CO.

Frank, C. B. (2002). *Heading the picture walk.* Presentation to fifth grade class at Capron Elementary School in Capron, IL.

Frank, C. B. (2004). *How to improve nonfiction reading for the ACT: Four-square reciprocal teaching template.* Presentation to teachers at Woodstock School District 200, Woodstock, IL.

Frase, L. T., & Schwartz, B. J. (1975). Effect on question production and answering on prose recall. *Journal of Educational Psychology, 67.*

Frayer, D., Frederick, W. G., & Klausmeier, H. (1969). *A schema for testing the level of cognitive mastery.* Working paper No. 16. Madison, WI: Wisconsin Research and Development.

Gallagher, P., & Norton, G. (2000). *A jumpstart to literacy: Using written conversation to help developing readers and writers.* Portsmouth, NH: Heinemann.

Gardener, H. (1983). *Multiple intelligences: The theory in practice.* New York: Basic Books.

Giles, J. (1987). *Ideas and insights: Language arts in the elementary schools.* National Council of Teachers of English.

Goodman, B. (2004). *English yes: Learning English*

through literature. Columbus, OH: Glencoe McGraw-Hill.

Gordon, C. J., & Pearson, P. D. (1983). *The effects of instruction in metacomprehension and inferencing on children's comprehension abilities* (Tech. Rep. No. 277). Urbana, IL: University of Illinois, Center for the Study of Reading.

Graves, D. (1983). *Writing: Teachers and children at work.* Portsmouth, NH: Heinemann.

Graves, J. F., & Slater, W. (1996). Vocabulary instruction in content areas. In D. Lapp, J. Flood, & N. Farnan, (Eds.). *Content area reading and learning: Instructional strategies.* Needham Heights, MA: Allyn & Bacon.

Graves, M., & Graves, B. (1994). *Scaffolding reading experiences: Designs for student success.* Norwood, MA: Christopher-Gordon.

Griggs, E., & Gil-Garcia, A. (2001). *What we know about helping middle and high school readers: Teaching learning strategies across the curriculum.* Arlington, VA: Educational Resource Service.

Grossi, J., & Frank, C. (2002). *Carousel brainstorming.* Presentation at Homewood School District 154, Homewood, IL.

Guice, B. M. (1969). The use of the cloze procedure for improving reading comprehension for college students. *Journal of Reading Behavior, 1,* 81–92.

Guthrie, J. R., Van Meter, P., McCann, A. D., Wigfield, A., Bennett, L., Poundstone, C. C. et al. (1995). Growth of literacy engagement: Changes in motivations and strategies during concept-oriented reading instruction. *Reading Research Quarterly, 31,* 306–332.

Haller, E., Child, D., & Walberg, H. J. (December, 1988). Can comprehension be taught: A quantitative synthesis. *Educational Researcher, 17, 9,* 5–8.

Halliday, M. A. K. (1978). *Language as social semiotic.* Baltimore, MD: University Park Press.

Halliday, M. A. K., & Hasan, R. (1976). *Cohesion in English.* New York: Longman.

Hancock, M. R. (1993). Exploring and extending personal response through literature journals. *Reading Teacher, 46,* 466–474.

Hansen, J., & Pearson, P. D. (1983). An instructional study: Improving the inferential comprehension of good and poor fourth-grade readers. *Journal of Educational Psychology, 75,* 821–829.

Harvey, S., & Goudvis, A. (2000). *Strategies that work: Teaching comprehension to enhance understanding.* Portland, ME: Stenhouse.

Hayes, D. (1989). Helping students GRASP the knack of writing summaries. *Journal of Reading,* 96–101.

Herber, H. (1970). *Teaching reading in content areas.* Englewood Cliffs, NJ: Prentice Hall.

Herber, H. (1978). *Teaching reading in content areas* (2nd ed.). Upper Saddle River, NJ: Prentice Hall.

Holston, V., & Santa, C. (1985). RAFT: A method of writing across the curriculum that works. *Journal of Reading, 28,* 456–457.

Howie, S. H. (1984). *A guidebook for teaching writing in content areas.* Boston: Allyn & Bacon.

Illinois State Board of Education. (1997). *Illinois learning standards.* Springfield, IL: Author.

Irwin, J. L. et al. (1995). *Enhancing social studies through literacy strategies.* Washington, DC: National Council for the Social Studies.

Jamestown Publishers. (1998). *The contempory reader.* Lincolnwood, IL: Jamestown Publishers.

Jewell, T., & Pratt, D. (1999). Literature discussions in the primary grades: Children's thoughtful discourse about books and what teachers can do to make it happen. *The Reading Teacher, 52,* 842–850.

Johnson, D. D., & Pearson, P .D. (1984). *Teaching reading vocabulary.* New York: Holt, Reinhart and Winston.

Johnson, D. D. M., Toms-Bronowski, S., & Pittelman, S. D. (1981). *An investigation of trends in vocabulary research and the effects of prior knowledge on instructional strategies for vocabulary acquisition.* (Theoretical Paper No. 95). Madison: Wisconsin Center for Educational Research.

Johnson D. W., & Johnson, R. (1985). The internal dynamics of cooperative learning groups. In R. Slavin, S. Sharan, S. Kagan, R. Lazarowitz, S. Webb, & R. Schmuck (Eds.), *Learning to cooperate, cooperating to learn* (pp. 103–124). New York: Plenum.

Kagan, S. (1989). *Cooperative Learning.* Resources for Teachers, 27134 Paseo Espada, 202 San Juan Capistrano, CA 92775.

Katz, C. (June, 1999). *Test learning strategies: Stop the process.* Presentation of Suburban Council of International Reading Association. Evanston, IL: National-Louis University.

Keene, E. O., & Zimmerman, S. (1997). *Mosaic of thought: Teaching comprehension in a readers' workshop.* Portsmouth, NH: Heinemann.

Kinkead, D., Thompson, R., Wright, C., & Gutierrez, C. (1992). Pyramiding: Reading and writing to learn social studies. *The Exchange, Secondary Reading Interest Group Newsletter, 5,* 2.

Kintsch, W., & Van Dijk, T. A. (1978). Toward a model of text comprehension and production. *Psychological Review, 85.*

Klein, J. (1988). *Teaching reading comprehension and vocabulary: A guide for teachers.* Englewood Cliffs, NJ: Prentice Hall.

Krull, K. (1993). *Lives of the musicians: Good times, bad times, and what the neighbors thought.* San Diego: Harcourt, Brace, Jovanovich.

Leu, Jr., D. S., & Leu, D. D. (2000).*Teaching with the internet: Lesson from the classroom* (3rd ed.). Norwood, MA: Christopher Gordon.

Maloch, B. (2002). Scaffolding student talk: One teachers role in literature discussion groups. *Reading Research Quarterly, 37, 1,* 94–112.

Maloch, B. (2002). Scaffolding student talk: One teacher's role in literature discussion groups. *Reading Research Quarterly, 37(1),* 94–112.

Manning, M., & Manning, G. (September, 1995). Reading and writing in the content areas. *Teaching K–8.*

Manz, S. L. (2002). A strategy for previewing textbooks:

Teaching readers to become THIEVES. *The Reading Teacher, 55*, 5, 434–436.

McGinley, W. J., & Denner P. R. (1987). Story impressions: A pre-reading/writing activity. *Journal of Reading, 31*, 248–253.

McKeown, M. G., & Beck, I. L. (1989). *The assessment and characterization of young learners' knowledge of a topic in history.* Paper presented at the National Reading Conference, San Antonio, TX.

Mercer, C. D., & Mercer, A. (1998). *Teaching students with learning problems.* Upper Saddle River, NJ: Prentice Hall.

Meyer, B. J. F., & Rice, E. (1984). The structure of text. In P. D. Pearson (Ed.), *Handbook of reading research* (pp. 319–352). New York: Longman.

Meyer, B. J. F., Brandt, D., & Bluth, G. (1980). Use of top-level structure in text: Key for reading comprehension of ninth-grade students. *Reading Research Quarterly, 6*, 72–103.

Mezynski, K. (1983). Issues concerning the acquisition of knowledge. Effects of vocabulary training on reading comprehension. *Review of Educational Research, 53*, 263–279.

Mosenthal, P. (1984). Reading comprehension research from a classroom perspective. In J. Flood (Ed.), *Promoting reading comprehension.* Newark, DE: International Reading Association.

Moore, D. W., Readance, J. E., & Rickelman, R. (1989). *Prereading activities for content area reading and learning* (2nd ed.). Newark, DE: International Reading Association.

Murray, D. M. (1987). *Writing to learn* (2nd ed.). New York: Holt, Rinehart and Winston.

Nagy, W. E., & Anderson, R. (1984). How many words are there in printed English? *Reading Research Quarterly, 19*, 304–330.

Nagy, W. E., & Herman, P. A. (1987). Depth and breadth of vocabulary knowledge: Implications for acquisition and instruction. In M. G. McKeown & M. E. Curtis, M. E. (Eds.). *The nature of vocabulary acquisition.* Hillsdale, NJ: Erlbaum.

National Council of Teachers of English. International Reading Association. (1996). *Standards for the English language arts.* Urbana, IL: National Council of Teachers of English, 27–46.

National Reading Panel. (2000). *Report of the National Reading Panel: Teaching children to read, an evidence-based assessment of the scientific research literature on reading and its implications for reading instruction.* Washington, DC: National Institute of Child Health and Development.

Newman, B. (1977). *The illustrated book of ballet stories.* New York: D. K. Publishing.

Niles, O. (1965). Organization perceived. In H. L. Herber (Ed.). *Developing study skills in secondary schools* (pp. 36–46). Newark, DE: International Reading Association.

Noden, H. R., & Vacca, R. T. (1994). *Whole language in middle and secondary classrooms.* New York: Harper Collins.

North Central Regional Educational Laboratory. (2000). *STRP handbook: Strategic teaching and reading project.* Naperville, IL: NCREL.

Palincsar, A., & Brown, A. (1984). Reciprocal teaching of comprehension fostering and comprehension monitoring activities. *Cognition and Instruction, 1*, 117–176.

Palmatier, R. (1973). A notetaking system for learning. *Journal of Reading, 17*, 36–39.

Paris, S. G., & Lindauer, B. K. (1976). The role of inference in children's comprehension and memory. *Cognitive Psychology, 8*, 217–227.

Pearson, P. D. (1985). Reading comprehension instruction: Six necessary steps. *Reading Teacher, 38*, 724–738.

Pearson, P. D., & Johnson, D. (1978). *Teaching reading comprehension.* Fort Worth, TX: Holt, Rinehart and Winston.

Pearson, P. D., Roehler, L. R., Dole, J. A., & Duffy, G. G. (1992). Developing expertise in reading comprehension: What should be taught and how should it be taught? In S. J. Samuels & A. Farstrup (Eds.), *What research has to say to the teacher of reading,* 2nd ed. Newark, DE: International Reading Association.

Pearson, P. D., Hanson, J., & Gordon, C. (1979). The effect of background on young children's comprehension of explicit and implicit information. *Journal of Reading Behavior, 11*, 201–210.

Piccolo, J. A. (1987). Expository text structure: Teaching and learning strategies. *The Reading Teacher, 40*, 838–847.

Raphael, T. E. (1986). Teaching question-answer relationships. *Reading Teacher, 39*, 516–520.

Rasinski, T. (2001). Handout entitled *Spinning straw into gold.* Reading Conference Presentation at Northern Illinois University.

Readence, J., Bean, T., & Baldwin, R. (1989). *Content area reading: An integrated approach* (3rd ed.). Dubuque, IA: Kendal/Hunt.

Redfield, D. L., & Roussear, E. W. (1981). Meta-Analysis of experimental research on teacher questioning behavior. *Review of Educational Research,* 51.

Richek, M., Caldwell, J., Jennings, J., & Lerner, J. (2002). *Reading problems: Assessment and teaching strategies.* Boston: Allyn & Bacon.

Riggs, E. G., & Gil-Garcia, A. (2001). *Helping middle and high school readers: Teaching and learning strategies across the curriculum.* Arlington, VA: Educational Research Service.

Robb, L. (2000). *Teaching reading in middle school: A strategic approach to teaching reading that improves comprehension and thinking.* New York: Scholastic.

Robinson, F. P. (1946). *Effective study.* New York: Harper-Collins.

Rosenblatt, L. M. (1978). *The reader, the text, the poem: The transactional theory of the literary work.* Carbondale, IL: Southern Illinois University.

Rubin, D. L. (1990). Introduction: Ways of thinking about talking and learning. In S. Hynds & D. L. Rubin (Eds.), *Perspectives on talk and learning* (pp. 1–17). Urbana, IL: National Council of Teachers of English.

Rumelhart, D. E. (1980). The building blocks of cognition. In R. J. Spiro, B. C. Bruce, & W. F. Brewer (Eds.). *Theoretical issues in reading comprehension*. Hillsdale, NJ: Erbaum.

Salisbury, R. (1934). A study of the transfer effects of training in logical organization. *Journal of Educational Research, 28,* 241–254.

Samuels, S. J., & Farstrup, A. E. (1992). *What research has to say about reading instruction,* 2nd ed. Newark, DE: International Reading Association.

Sanders, S. (1997). *A place called freedom.* New York: Atheneum.

Santa, C., Havens, L., & Valdes, B. (2004). *Project CRISS: Creating independence through student-owned strategies.* Dubuque, IA: Kendall Hunt.

Santa, C. M. (1988). *Content reading including study systems.* Dubuque, IA: Kendal Hunt.

Schacter, S. W. (1978). *An investigation of the effects of vocabulary instruction and schemata orientation on reading comprehension.* Doctoral Dissertation, University of Minnesota.

Schwartz, R., & Raphael, T. (1985). Concept of definition: A key to improving students' vocabulary. *The Reading Teacher, 39,* 676–682.

Shanahan, T. (Ed.). (1990). *Reading and writing together: New perspectives for the classroom.* Norwood, MA: Christopher-Gordon.

Short, K., Kaufman, G., Kaser, S., Kahn, L., & Crawford, K. (1999). Teacher watching: Examining teacher talk in literature circles. *Language Arts, 76,* 377–385.

Slavin, R. (1980). Cooperative learning. *Review of Educational Research, 50.*

Slavin, R. E. (1988). Cooperative learning and student achievement. In R. E. Slavin (Ed.), *School and classroom organization.* Hillsdale, NJ: Erlbaum.

Smith, N. B. (1964). Patterns of writing in different subject areas. *Journal of Reading, 7,* 31–37.

Solon, C. (1980). The pyramid diagram: A college study skills tool. *Journal of Reading, 23,* 7.

Speare, E. G. (1983). *The sign of the beaver.* New York: Dell.

Stahl, S., & Fairbanks, M. (1986). The effects of vocabulary instruction. A model-based meta-analysis. *Review of Educational Research, 56,* 72–110.

Stahl, S., & Kapinus, B. (1991). Possible sentences: Predicting word meanings to teach content area vocabulary. *The Reading Teacher, 45,* 36–43.

Stahl, S. A. (1985). To teach a word well: A framework for vocabulary instruction. *Reading World, 24*(3), 16–27.

Stanfield, D., Grossi, J., & Frank, C. (2002). Professional development focuses on learning strategies for content area reading. *ERS Sucessful School Practices, 22,* 1, 1–5.

Stanfill, S. (1978). The great American one-sentence summary. In O. Clapp (Ed.), *Classroom practices in teaching classroom English, 1977–1978* (pp. 47–49). Urbana, IL: National Council of Teachers of English.

Stauffer, R. G. (1969). *Directing reading maturity as a cognitive process.* New York: Harper and Row.

Sternberg, R. (1987). What does it mean to be smart? *Educational Leadership, 54*(6), 20–24.

Strickland, C., & Boswell, J. (1995). *The annotated Mona Lisa.* Kansas City: Universal Press.

Taba, H. (1967). *Teacher's handbook for elementary social studies.* Reading, MA: Addison-Wesley.

Terman, L. M. (1916). *The measurement of intelligence.* Boston: Houghton Mifflin.

Tierney, R., & Shanahan, T. (1991). Research on reading-writing relationship: Interactions, transactions, and outcomes. In D. Pearson et al. (Eds), *Handbook of Reading Research, Volume 2* (pp. 246–280). New York: Longman.

Tierney, R. J., & Pearson, P. D. (1983). Toward composing a model of reading. *Language Arts, 60,* 568–580.

Tierney, R. J., Readence, J. E., & Dishner, E. K. (1980). *Reading strategies and practices: A guide for improving instruction.* Boston: Allyn & Bacon.

Tompkins, G. (1997). *Literacy for the 21st century: A balanced approach.* New York: Prentice Hall.

Tompkins, G. E. (1994). *Teaching writing: Balancing process and product,* 2nd ed. New York: Macmillan.

U.S. Department of Education. (2001). *Put reading first: The research blocks for teaching children to read.* Washington, DC: Partnership for Reading.

Vacca, R., & Vacca, J. (1996). *Content area reading.* New York: Harper Collins.

Vacca, R., & Vacca, J. (1999). *Content area reading.* New York: Longman.

Vacca, R., & Vacca, J. (2005). *Content area reading: Literacy and learning across the curriculum.* Boston: Pearson Education, Inc.

Vallaume, S. K., Worden, T., Williams, S., Hopkins, L., & Rosenblatt, C. (1994). Five teachers in search of a discussion. *The Reading Teacher, 47,* 480–487.

Vygotsky, L. S. (1978). *Mind in society: The development of higher psychological processes.* In M. Cole, V. John-Steiner, S. Scribner, & E. Souberman (Eds.). Cambridge, MA: Harvard University Press.

Whipple, G. (Ed.). (1925). *The twenty-fourth yearbook of the National Society for the Study of Education: Report of the National Committee on Reading.* Bloomington, IL: Public School Publishing Company.

Wixson, K. (1983). Questions about a text: What you ask about is what children learn. *The Reading Teacher, 37.*

Index